The Complete Guide to Yorkshire Terriers

Dr. Jo de Klerk

LP Media Inc. Publishing

Text copyright © 2019 by LP Media Inc.

All rights reserved.

No part of this book may be reproduced or transmitted in any form or by any means, electronic or mechanical, including photocopying, recording, or by an information storage and retrieval system - except by a reviewer who may quote brief passages in a review to be printed in a magazine or newspaper - without permission in writing from the publisher. For information address LP Media Inc. Publishing, 3178 253rd Ave. NW, Isanti, MN 55040

www.lpmedia.org

Publication Data

Dr. Jo de Klerk

The Complete Guide to Yorkshire Terriers ---- First edition.

Summary: "Successfully raising a Yorkshire Terrier dog from puppy to old age" --- Provided by publisher.

ISBN: 978-1-79-558752-5

[1. Yorkshire Terriers --- Non-Fiction] I. Title.

This book has been written with the published intent to provide accurate and authoritative information in regard to the subject matter included. While every reasonable precaution has been taken in preparation of this book the author and publisher expressly disclaim responsibility for any errors, omissions, or adverse effects arising from the use or application of the information contained inside. The techniques and suggestions are to be used at the reader's discretion and are not to be considered a substitute for professional veterinary care. If you suspect a medical problem with your dog, consult your veterinarian.

Design by Sorin Rădulescu

First paperback edition, 2019

TABLE OF CONTENTS

THE COMPLETE GUIDE TO YORKSHIRE TERRIERS
By Dr. Jo de Klerk 7

CHAPTER 1
Breed Overview 8
About the Breed 8
Looks 8
Age Expectancy 9
Personality 10
Out of the Home 11
In the Home 11
Costs of Keeping a Yorkshire Terrier 13

CHAPTER 2
Breed History 14
Origin of the Breed 14
Genetic Origins 15
Historical Standards 17
Famous Yorkshire Terriers of the Past 18

CHAPTER 3
Behavior 20
Temperament 20
Trainability 22
Snapping 24
Separation Anxiety 24
Importance of Socialization 27
Exercise Needs 28

CHAPTER 4
Preparations for a New Dog 30
Preparing Your Home 30
Shopping List for Your New Dog 33
Introducing Your New Yorkshire Terrier to Your Other Dogs 35
Introducing Your New Yorkshire Terrier to Children 37

CHAPTER 5
How to Choose a Yorkshire Terrier **38**
Purchasing or Rescuing?. 38
Researching the Establishment 40
Inquire about Parents 42
Looking at the Puppy. 43
Behavioral and Health Considerations with a Rescue Dog 45

CHAPTER 6
Training **46**
Toilet Training 48
How to Teach Sit. 50
How to Teach Stay 51
How to Teach Lie Down 52
How to Teach to Walk on the Leash 53
How to Teach to Walk off the Leash/Recall 53
Agility. 55

CHAPTER 7
Traveling **56**
Preparations for Travel 56
Traveling in a Car 58
Traveling by Plane. 60
Vacation Lodging 61
Leaving Your Dog at Home 61

CHAPTER 8
Nutrition. **64**
Importance of Nutrition. 64
Commercial Food 65
BARF and Homemade Diets 66
Pet Food Labels 67
Weight Monitoring 69

CHAPTER 9
Dental Care **72**
Importance of Dental Care 72
Dental Anatomy 73
Breed-Specific Dental Issues 73
Dental Care. 76
Dental Procedures 78

CHAPTER 10
Grooming ... 80
About the Coat ... 80
Coat Health ... 82
External Parasites ... 84
Nail Clipping ... 85
Ear Cleaning ... 86
Anal Glands ... 87

CHAPTER 11
Preventative Veterinary Medicine ... 88
Choosing a Veterinarian ... 88
Vaccinations ... 89
Microchipping ... 91
Neutering ... 91
Internal Parasites ... 93
Pet Insurance ... 94

CHAPTER 12
Yorkshire Terrier Diseases ... 96
Dry Eye ... 96
Patella Luxation ... 98
Collapsed Trachea ... 99
Skin Allergies ... 99

CHAPTER 13
Breeding ... 102
Deciding about Breeding ... 102
Mating ... 103
Pregnancy ... 103
Birthing ... 104
Aftercare ... 105
Raising Puppies ... 107

CHAPTER 14
Showing ... 108
Selecting a Dog for Showing ... 109
After Selecting Your Puppy ... 110
Breed Standard ... 112
Preparing for a Show ... 116

CHAPTER 15
Living with a Senior Dog 118
Diet Change 119
Senior Wellness Checks 120
Arthritis 121
Dementia 123
Organ Deterioration 124
Loss of Senses 125
Bladder Control 126
Saying Goodbye 127

ACKNOWLEDGMENTS 128

THE COMPLETE GUIDE TO YORKSHIRE TERRIERS
By Dr. Jo de Klerk

Yorkshire Terriers are among the top ten most popular breeds in America, and it's easy to see why. They are loyal, lovable, and playful and make perfect pets for first-time dog owners. This book provides all you need to know about how to look after the breed, whether you are buying a Yorkshire Terrier as a pet, show dog, or breeding dog.

In The Complete Guide to Yorkshire Terriers you will learn all about the ideal nutrition for the breed, training strategies, traveling, breed predisposed diseases, grooming, dental care, preventative veterinary care, neutering, and senior care. All information is specific to Yorkshire Terriers and presented in easy-to-read but comprehensive detail, ensuring there is nothing left for you to wonder or worry about.

The book will give you vital information about purchasing and rescue options, as well as top tips for when you bring your Yorkshire Terrier home for the first time. It will guide you from the exciting time before you get your puppy, all the way through to when it's time to say goodbye to your old and beloved friend.

The book is compiled by veterinarian Dr. Jo de Klerk and will provide you with all you need to know about the breed and more. Whether you are a first-time Yorkshire Terrier owner, professional dog owner, or first-time dog owner altogether, there is something for everyone to help you bond and care for your new little friend.

CHAPTER 1
Breed Overview

About the Breed

The Yorkshire Terrier is a small breed dog with a feisty and friendly nature. Although they can vary in size according to their breeding, they are considered to belong in the Toy breed category. Toy breeds are often referred to as lap dogs, and a widely held perception is that they are "old ladies' dogs"; however, this label misrepresents their large personalities and fearless attitude. There is a lot more to a Yorkie than the common stereotype.

Even within the same litter, there may be wide variation in the size of the Yorkshire Terrier, and the adult dog may range from 4 pounds to as much as 15 pounds. Especially small "teacup"-sized Yorkies have been unnaturally bred and may be predisposed to more health problems than the standard dog, which should be considered when making a purchasing decision.

Looks

The Yorkshire Terrier in its natural state has a fine, long coat in two main colors that are usually referred to as "Steel Blue and Tan," but may vary from silver to black and from honey beige to rich tan. The coat comes in two types. The silk coat, which hangs straight, will grow to the floor unless clipped, and will need to be tied back or trimmed away from the eyes, whereas, the wavy coat is shorter and scruffier. The Yorkie has no undercoat and little dander in the coat, which makes the breed suitable for allergy sufferers, but consequently the dog feels the cold and should not be kept outdoors in a cold climate. Their head is small and their muzzle is of medium length. There are two variations in the ears. Most Yorkies have pricked ears, but some may have ear flaps. The back is level and the tail is carried half-down, except when used expressively in greeting or to acknowledge anything exciting, when it may be held high and wagged vigorously.

CHAPTER 1 Breed Overview

Age Expectancy

The life expectancy of a Yorkshire Terrier is quite high at 14–16 years, and this should certainly be considered if choosing a puppy. Although the Yorkshire Terrier copes well with indoor living and is an excellent companion, the exercise needs of the breed should not be underestimated, so the owner should think ahead to their own fitness in future years, and what arrangements they might put in place if they encounter mobility problems or if the dog should outlive them. Because of the breed's longevity and popularity with older people, Yorkshire Terriers may often be found in shelters or rehomed privately in later life, so homing an adult dog may be a better alternative than buying a puppy for some people. In these instances, the adult dog may come ready trained and with the calm temperament of seniority, or with baggage from a bad start, and careful consideration should be made as to the individual circumstance and whether the new owner is suited to the dog's needs.

Photo Courtesy of Mike Voigts

Personality

"Yorkies are very intelligent, witty, and can bring much laugher to your home."

Elaine Schneider
High 'N Yorkies

Yorkshire Terriers are surprisingly energetic and enthusiastic by nature, and their lively personalities should be appreciated, so a potential owner looking for a quiet life may wish to reconsider the choice of a Yorkshire Terrier. They can be quite vocal if they pick up on noises or activity outside the four walls of their home. While the Yorkie is in many ways suited to living in an apartment due to its size, consideration should be made to the thickness of the walls and the likelihood of disturbing other neighbors. It is always a sad outcome for a dog and its owner if rehoming becomes necessary due to nuisance behavior, which in many countries is legally enforceable.

This being said, with diligent training of a puppy, or with prudent selection of a suitable rescue dog, a Yorkshire Terrier may be an excellent choice for those living in close proximity to other neighbors, especially as the breed is non-aggressive and unlikely to be seen as a threat.

Although the Yorkshire Terrier is friendly by nature, it may be reactive with children who do not respect its space or who pull its ears, coat, or tail. To avoid the possibility of the Yorkie snapping defensively in these instances, it is important that children are taught to be gentle with this sensitive breed, in which case there is every chance that a good relationship will blossom between child and dog. When each understand and trust the other, Yorkies are often known to help dog-phobic children to overcome their fears, as their size and appearance are appealing to children.

> **HELPFUL TIP**
> **The Perfect Lapdog**
>
> An ideal dog for city dwellers, Yorkshire Terriers require moderate exercise and are small in stature. Weighing in at approximately seven lbs. and with a height of seven to eight inches on average, this member of the toy group is the ultimate lapdog. Life expectancy for Yorkies is between 11-15 years. Although no dog breeds are 100 percent hypoallergenic, Yorkies come very close according to the American Kennel Club. Yorkies have "hair," not fur, and are non-shedding which makes them comfortable housemates for those with allergies. The Yorkshire Terrier often ranks in the top ten of the over 200 dog breeds recognized by the AKC.

CHAPTER 1 Breed Overview

Out of the Home

Photo Courtesy of Jodi Boerema

The owner should consider the outdoor needs of the Yorkshire Terrier and be able to take the dog out daily for at least one dedicated walk of half an hour. Alternatively, the pup could accompany the owner on their day-to-day activities. Walking the Yorkie benefits its overall health and fitness as well as providing an opportunity for socialization, sniffing, and exercising its animal instincts. Recall training is essential if the dog is to be walked off the leash, as Yorkies like to chase small animals. Their feisty nature also comes to the fore when confronting other dogs of any size, as the Yorkie has no concept of his own small stature. Whereas these encounters are usually good-natured and a good opportunity for play, the owner should be aware that the Yorkshire Terrier can get into trouble by provoking larger, more aggressive dogs, in which he could come off worse due to his size. The Yorkie should be kept under control in public spaces and the owner should be vigilant in reading the temperament of the other dogs sharing the same area.

In the Home

Photo Courtesy of Billie Jean Gaskin

Compared to other breeds, the Yorkshire Terrier has very little detrimental effect on the cleanliness of the home. It is a non-shedding breed that leaves little hair behind, does not drool, and tends to stay clean on walks. Regular grooming will ensure that any loose hair is brushed out and will not transfer to furniture.

Whereas some Yorkies may be destructive in the home, this is not a breed characteristic, and training or preventative measures, such as crating when out, may address undesired behavior if it presents

Photo Courtesy of Sean O'Meara

as an issue. Housebreaking is important and whereas the Yorkie has a reputation for being hard to housebreak, the owner should expect success with patient and consistent training.

The Yorkshire Terrier loves company and should not be left for long periods. It may be worth considering having two dogs (either two Yorkies or two different breeds) for companionship when the owner is out of the house. A male and female pairing are considered the best partnership, although if breeding is not on the agenda then the male should be castrated and the female spayed too. These measures will also protect the hygiene of the home as well as avoiding sexually driven behavior with other dogs in public areas.

The Yorkshire Terrier can also get on well with other pets such as cats, though socialization is best achieved at an early age. An adult dog rehomed from a shelter may already be socialized with cats or other pets, but in these cases each dog should be considered on their individual merits as retraining may be more challenging later in life as well as stressful for the dog.

Costs of Keeping a Yorkshire Terrier

Although the Yorkshire Terrier may be predisposed to certain ailments which will be discussed in a later chapter, they are a relatively low-cost breed, being largely healthy with low feed costs. When considering the cost of keeping a dog, however, both regular and unforeseen veterinary expenses should be factored in, and pet insurance is a wise precaution.

It can be very rewarding to share your life and your home with a Yorkshire Terrier, and it is no surprise that Yorkie owners can become very passionate about the breed, and may own several Yorkies, either at any one time, or successively. In the light of many common misconceptions, learning more about what to expect from owning a Yorkie is the first step to a friendship for life.

CHAPTER 2
Breed History

In order to understand why the Yorkshire Terrier isn't your typical passive lap dog, it is important to understand a little about the background of the breed, its genetics, and the original purpose for which it was bred.

Origin of the Breed

Typically of working terriers, the name is a clue as to the origin of the breed. There are no prizes for guessing that the Yorkshire Terrier was developed in Yorkshire, in the north of England. In the nineteenth century, Yorkshire was a county at the heart of the industrial revolution, and in order to control the rat problem in the mines and cotton mills, a fearless, prey-driven small-breed terrier was required to keep industrial workspaces clear of vermin. In addition, the Yorkie found employment in more rural areas, carried in hunters' pockets to burrow after badgers and foxes. The bravery of this little dog in the face of potentially much larger animals certainly doesn't sound like your typical pampered, home-loving pooch, and it's consequently important to understand that the Yorkie does not fit the commonly held stereotype.

Photo Courtesy of Nadia du Toit.

CHAPTER 2   Breed History

Genetic Origins

The primary breeds that made up the first Yorkshire Terriers were Scottish, as Yorkshire was at that time a huge draw for the Scottish workforce who brought their working terriers with them. The varieties in the Yorkshire Terrier gene pool continue to be a subject for debate, but are usually agreed to be the Clydesdale Terrier, the Waterside Terrier (otherwise known as the Otter Terrier), and the Old English Terrier. These three breeds are now extinct. The Skye Terrier is often credited with being an ancestor of the Yorkie. This is correct insofar as the Clydesdale is a blue and tan silky-coated variant of the Skye, and the favored coloration for the Yorkshire Terrier breed. The Paisley Terrier, on the other hand, is an all-blue version of the Skye and another contributing variant.

> **FUN FACT**
> **"The Weaver Dog"**
>
> The breed was developed in the mid 1800s in the counties of Yorkshire and Lancashire in Northern England. These small, compact dogs took on the difficult job of running among the wool looms in Scotland, pursuing rodents and acquiring the nickname "Weaver Dogs." Coal miners also utilized Yorkies as "exterminators" in the coal mines. They are true terriers, having maintained this character trait since their development. The Kennel Club (England) first recognized the breed in 1886.

The first Yorkies were not known by the name "Yorkshire Terrier" until 1870, prior to which they had acquired the name "Broken-haired Scotch Terrier." But as their breeding was refined in Yorkshire, one show commentator suggested they should adopt the name of their home county, and hence the Yorkshire Terrier became the proud ambassador for Yorkshire.

In the early days, the Yorkshire Terrier was diverse in its defining characteristics, but in the 1860s, a Yorkshire woman, Mary Ann Foster, entered her Paisley-type Yorkshire Terrier into the show ring, and Huddersfield Ben, as the dog was called, became the breed standard. His performance at stud led him to be referred to as the "father of the breed," or foundation sire.

Huddersfield Ben was born in 1865. His sire was Mr. Boscovitch's Dog, and his dam was Eastwood's Lady. Both parents had been linebred, which refers to a mother-son pairing. This breed-refinement led to him becoming a popular show champion, winning 74 prizes in dog shows, as well as competing in ratting contests. He was relatively large in size at 9–12 pounds, but he regularly sired dogs that were able to compete under the seven-pound limit. He is credited with producing most of the foundation stock of the breed, even though he only lived to six years of age, when he was killed under the wheels of a carriage.

Paintings of Huddersfield Ben show a stocky square-set dog with a long back and a silky coat falling to knee-height. His ears are pricked and his long fringe falls across his eyes. His muzzle also sports a long moustache. He certainly looks every inch the grandsire of the breed.

During the later Victorian era, following the success of Huddersfield Ben, the Yorkshire Terrier became a popular contender in the show ring, where its luxuriant coat, small size, and companionable character caught the attention of the upper classes. Consequently, the Yorkshire Terrier became a fashionable household pet and a status symbol. In this capacity, the breed soon made its way to other parts of the world, particularly British settlements, as migrant Britons took their constant companions with them, where their appeal ensured that they would continue to flourish in countries such as South Africa, Australia, New Zealand, Canada, and the USA. The United States in particular took the breed to its heart and The Yorkshire Terrier Club of America was founded in 1915, prior to which Yorkies had been bred in America for over 40 years.

CHAPTER 2 Breed History

Photo Courtesy of Jaime Thurman

Historical Standards

By 1890, the show standard was set. Of the coat, the standard reads: "The hair should be as long and straight as possible (not wavy) which should be flossy not woolly. It should extend from the back of the head to the root of the tail. Color a bright steel blue and on no account intermingled with fawn or dark hair.

"The very long hair at the muzzle should be a rich, deep tan not intermingled with any sooty or gray. Under the chin long hair about the same color as on the crown of the head which should be a golden tan and not on any account intermingled with dark sooty hairs. Hair on sides of the head should be very long, a few shades deeper tan than the top of the head especially about the ear roots."

Of the tail, the 1890 standard reads it should be: "Cut to medium length, with plenty of hair darker in blue color than the rest of the body especially at the end of the tail, and carried a little higher than the level of the back." And of the ears, before the outlawing of ear-cropping, the 1890 standard reads: "Ears cut or uncut, quite erect: uncut, small V-shaped, and carried semi-erect covered with short hair. Color to be a deep, dark tan."

The general appearance of the Yorkshire Terrier in 1890 is certainly not unlike the show breed that we recognize today: "This should be of a long-coated pet dog, the coat hanging quite straight and evenly down each side, a parting extending from the nose to the end of the tail. The animal should be compact and neat, the carriage being very 'sprightly' bearing an important air. Although its frame is hidden beneath a mantle of hair the general outline should be such as to suggest the existence of a vigorous and well-proportioned body ... Weight divided into two classes, under five pounds and over five pounds, but not to exceed twelve pounds."

Famous Yorkshire Terriers of the Past

Evidence of the Yorkie's continuing popularity at the turn of the century is found in the original illustrations for L. Frank Baum's book version of The Wonderful Wizard of Oz. In the story, published in 1900, Dorothy's dog, Toto, as drawn by W.W. Denslow who owned a Yorkie, appears to be unmistakably a Yorkshire Terrier, even though the breed is not stated explicitly in the story, only referred to as "a little black dog with long silky hair." As Yorkies are the only terriers with silky coats, and together with the evidence of the illustrations, it can reasonably be assumed Toto was a Yorkie, although in the film version, the role went to a female wire-haired Cairn Terrier.

Just as the popularity of the Yorkie was beginning to drop in the 1940s, another celebrity dog by the name of Smoky came to the rescue. In 1944, during World War II, a group of American troops discovered Smoky in an abandoned foxhole in New Guinea. She was clearly an intelligent and spirited dog, but appeared to understand neither English nor Japanese, giving no clues as to her previous owners. However, she had a gift for entertainment and performing tricks, a skillset that was put to good use as a new recruit – transporting a telegraph wire 70 feet through a narrow eight-inch pipe that was partially blocked with mud and debris, an achievement that her diminutive size of only seven inches in height and four pounds in weight, not to mention her courage and determination, made possible.

Despite her size, Smoky was a resilient little dog, living in very challenging conditions in the equatorial jungle with the American troops, surviving air raids, gunfire, and typhoons without illness or injury. She even

CHAPTER 2 Breed History

Photo Courtesy of Sean O'Meara

parachuted 30 feet out of a tree. On her return to civilian life, Smoky became a sensation and an early television star, performing tricks such as walking a tightrope while blindfolded. It is true to say that Smoky's life was a long way removed from a boudoir cushion, and shows that the capabilities of a Yorkshire Terrier should never be underestimated. Indeed, although some of her tricks may not have been strictly necessary for the war effort, those who claim a Yorkshire Terrier is untrainable should remember Smoky and her working predecessors.

During the latter part of the twentieth century, the Yorkshire Terrier enjoyed a popularity revival, often appearing under the arms of celebrities and in the movies. In 1978, Champion Cede Higgins was the first Yorkshire Terrier to win Best in Show at the Westminster Kennel Club dog show, and in 1997, Champion Ozmilion Mystification won Best in Show at Crufts; the first Yorkie to take the title at the world's biggest and most prestigious dog show.

From its origins in mid-nineteenth-century England as a working dog, to its fluctuating popularity as a companion, today the Yorkshire Terrier features in the top ten of all breeds, loved by owners across the world, and is firmly here to stay.

CHAPTER 3
Behavior

"Stress does affect Yorkies. They do not do well with stress. Stress for them is often due to a change in their routine. Too much change can cause them to have gastrointestinal problems and should be addressed with your trusted veterinarian as soon as symptoms present themselves."

Marsha
Miracle Yorkies

Temperament

As already discussed, the Yorkshire Terrier was bred originally as a ratter, and even after 150 years, its original instincts are still intact. As a working dog, the Yorkie had to be tenacious, fearless, and not afraid to confront potentially larger animals. Consequently, for a little dog, the Yorkshire Terrier has a big personality, with an alert intelligence and lively spirit.

Yorkie owners in rural and semi-rural locations will soon discover that their dog will be unable to help themselves when catching sight of a squirrel or rodent, and in these situations, recall training can be very hard to enforce. This is simply the natural instinct of the Yorkshire Terrier coming to the fore as a reminder that he did not originate in a lady's parlor, but in the industrial north of England with a job to do.

However, this former working dog certainly proved adaptable to life as a companion, enjoying the indulgencies of a

> **QUOTE**
> *"And though she be but little, she is fierce."*
>
> Feisty, sometimes bossy, and very loyal, Yorkies are small in stature but have large personalities. Although not guaranteed to produce love and laughter, Yorkies are often at the top of the "favorite dog" list. Yorkies can become territorial, so socialization is important. Get your puppy out to mingle with other dogs and people as early and as often as possible to ensure a well-mannered companion.

CHAPTER 3 Behavior

Photo Courtesy of Manuela Duarte

pampered existence, and becoming fiercely loyal to his or her owner. The capacity of the Yorkie to form a bond with its human has consolidated its place in the world's affections. The Yorkie can, however, be quite possessive of its owner's attentions and protective in spite of its size. If this character trait is allowed to become engrained through lack of socialization with other human beings, for example if the owner is reclusive, then it is easy to understand why the breed has acquired a reputation for being unfriendly and difficult. This is not the natural temperament of a Yorkie, but it can become a one-person dog in a confined living environment.

Trainability

"Some Yorkies will overwhelm you with kindness, jumping up and down on you, just as with any other breed. Reward good behavior and ignore bad behavior. Pet them and love on them when they are calm and sitting or lying down, and ignore when they jump on you. You can gently push them down, but it is useless to continue to reprimand them verbally as that is just giving them the attention they are seeking. Most dogs look at yelling as being out of control. They view it as barking. So it's best to use simple calm words and some hand signals."

Marsha
Miracle Yorkies

The Yorkshire Terrier is an intelligent dog, and certainly not untrainable as some people claim. Its background in the mills and mines as well as in the field, together with the examples of highly trained dogs such as Smoky (mentioned in chapter 2), should underline the fact that Yorkies are highly capable of learning.

Photo Courtesy of Mike Voigts

It is important for the dog's own safety, as well as for its future welfare, that the Yorkshire Terrier should be trained, and there is no good reason to be defeatist about training a Yorkie. Training will be more successful if the owner expects success, as they will be more positive and persistent in achieving it. For this reason, negative stereotyping is not helpful, especially as it is unfounded in the case of the Yorkshire Terrier.

As with any domestic dog, in expecting the Yorkshire Terrier to live inside our homes and obey our rules, we are asking it to subvert some of its own animal instincts. If

CHAPTER 3 Behavior

Photo Courtesy of Sophie Thackray

in the training process there are setbacks, such as soiling or destructive behavior, this is not the dog being naughty, it is merely that sufficient time is needed for it to learn a new way of life. It is because of the dog's ability to bond with a human and adopt its lifestyle that it is the most domesticated of all animals, and known as Man's Best Friend.

As with any breed, it is easier to train the Yorkshire Terrier to modify its natural behavior in order to live in our homes if the owner is working with a puppy. Older dogs that have been poorly trained may have engrained behaviors that are harder to eradicate and may require the help of a professional behaviorist. However, the Yorkie is a dog that wants to please, and with patience and understanding will soon pick up on what is being asked of it, and will enthusiastically embrace the lifestyle of its human best friend.

Snapping

As we have already mentioned, the Yorkshire Terrier can be very protective of their human, and may be defensive if approached by a stranger that they perceive as a threat. In this case, the dog has adopted a position of dominance and assumes it is his role to guard. Even a small dog like a Yorkie can be a Rottweiler inside their head if they have not learned that their owner is in charge.

Another reason a Yorkie may snap is out of fear, for example if he perceives that he may get hurt by the insensitive attention of children poking or pulling him, or if he has become conditioned to being stepped on by careless adults. In this case, he is simply defending himself from injury, and the owner should be aware of what is causing fear in their Yorkshire Terrier and learn conditioning techniques to help their dog deal with threatening situations without resorting to snapping. Of course, as fear is a learned behavior, it is prudent to anticipate situations, such as the examples given, and ensure that they do not happen in the first place.

It is important to realize that snapping is not biting. It is a warning and is not indicative of aggression. The owner should learn about the dog's body language to gauge true aggression, which is not a natural breed trait of the Yorkshire Terrier. This knowledge can also be useful to spot in other dogs, to ensure that the Yorkie does not become embroiled in a fight in which he may come off worse.

Separation Anxiety

The Yorkshire Terrier can become extremely attached to their human, and find it unbearable to be separated from them for any period of time. In most instances, this is not helpful, as despite being a portable size, the Yorkie cannot possibly accompany their owner on every outing outside the home.

A dog experiencing separation anxiety may pace, bark, whine, scratch at doors and carpets, or destroy objects such as toys and furniture. In the process, the dog may actually harm themselves. The claws, paws, and mouth may suffer injury or they may hurt themselves in frantic behavior jumping on and off furniture. Consequently, for the welfare of the dog as well as to avoid damage to the home and neighborly relations, separation anxiety needs to be addressed if it should occur.

If the owner is unsure as to whether their dog is experiencing separation anxiety, the purchase of a dog-cam will allow them to see what

CHAPTER 3   Behavior

their Yorkshire Terrier gets up to when they are not at home. This may be better or worse than expected, as some dogs settle after an initial period of stress, whereas others may become progressively anxious.

One cause of separation anxiety is over-dependence on the owner, and therefore at the puppy stage it is important for the owner not to give in to the temptation to take the puppy everywhere with them, but to start conditioning them to short periods alone. In the initial stages, these periods may be no more than a few minutes, but can be built up over a longer period to a recommended maximum of four hours. The important factor in leaving a dog is that the owner should not fuss over the dog either on leaving or on their return. In these instances, the dog believes separation is a big deal and they are right to be anxious. But if the owner leaves calmly and ignores the dog on their initial return, the dog accepts the situation as normal and nothing to worry about.

Owners may find it helpful to redirect destructive behavior in their absence by providing a suitable toy, such as a Kong, which may be stuffed with wet dog food, pâté, or xylitol-free peanut butter. Not only does this provide a distraction, but chewing releases endorphins which help to relax the dog. It is not advisable to give a dog chews that require supervision, such as rawhide or knucklebone, to avoid the risk of choking when no one is on hand to respond.

It may also be helpful to leave the radio or television on when the owner is out of the home. This can create the impression of human company but also drown out noises outside the home that may create anxiety in the dog when they are alone.

In order to preempt the possibility of separation anxiety, it is also worth considering a canine companion for your Yorkshire Terrier so that he is never completely alone. Most Yorkies respond very well to having the companionship of another dog, Yorkie or otherwise, especially if conditioned to this as a puppy. Litter-mates may get on especially well together. If homing two dogs of different genders, it is important they should be neutered unless they are to be intentionally bred from, as a Yorkshire Terrier female may come into season as early as four months, so the male should be castrated prior to this. Rescue dogs will have to be assessed on their individual circumstances, as some may be unable to tolerate other dogs, in which case the shelter will rehome them accordingly.

Rescue dogs may require a longer period of rehabilitation from separation anxiety, as they may be harboring experiences of being abandoned. They do not have the trust that their owner will return. In these cases, patience and understanding may rebuild their trust, but often particularly affected dogs will only be rehomed to households where someone is at home most of the day.

If separation anxiety continues to be a problem, there are products on the market that claim to soothe dogs by releasing a dog-appeasing pheromone, or DAP. This simulates the pheromone released by the mother to calm her puppies after birth. The product is available as a plug-in, a spray, or a collar. Tablets or dry dog biscuits are also available containing casein, which occurs in the mother's milk to relax her puppies, or L-tryptophan, which increases the well-being hormone serotonin in the brain.

As a last resort, a dog behaviorist may be consulted if problems persist. The owner should not feel defeated if they need the advice of a professional. It is the sensible next stage to helping their dog so that both dog and owner can enjoy a stress-free relationship and the rewards that owning a Yorkshire Terrier brings.

CHAPTER 3   Behavior

Importance of Socialization

It has been mentioned previously that the Yorkshire Terrier should be socialized with other humans, to avoid being a one-person dog with all the undesirable behaviors that brings. But of equal importance is that the Yorkie should be socialized with other dogs. This can begin after the puppy's initial vaccination course is complete, and puppy training classes are an excellent idea, because not only does the dog meet a variety of breeds at the same life stage in a controlled environment, but the owner receives moral and professional support in guiding their dog through this early and important step in life.

The best way to find out about puppy socialization classes in your area is to ask your local veterinarian, as they will have a list and contact details. Puppy classes may even be held at the vet practice. In other locations they may be the kindergarten stage before dog training classes, which is an excellent way for the new owner to feel supported through

the early months, and for the dog to make friends that they may keep in contact with for life.

If the owner does not have a local puppy class, or wishes to socialize their dog on their own terms, the park is the obvious place for the puppy to meet new friends. The Yorkshire Terrier will also enjoy sniffing smells left by other dogs and wildlife, and in leaving his own mark. As mentioned previously, the owner should always be mindful in public spaces that not all reactive dogs will be under control or muzzled, and a lively Yorkie puppy may provoke a response that he is ill-equipped to deal with. Therefore, introductions should proceed with caution and with the cooperation of the other owner. One rule of thumb is the three-second-rule: if the dogs continue to stare each other down without a positive engagement, then at three seconds the owner should walk their dog away before a confrontation occurs. A bad experience as a puppy can engrain fear for life, or permanent emotional or physical damage, but positive experiences are the building blocks for a happy and confident dog with the skillset to enjoy life to the full.

Exercise Needs

Although the Yorkshire Terrier is small and has the common reputation of being a cosseted indoor dog with no exercise needs, this is a misconception. The Yorkie has energy in abundance that needs to be channeled into regular physical activity for the good of his body and his mind.

Just like us, the Yorkshire Terrier needs exercise to keep him fit, and a daily walk can be beneficial for dog and owner alike, and a good incentive for the owner to take care of their own health as much as that of their dog. Dogs that stay in good shape are less likely to suffer joint issues, diabetes, and even some cancers. For the Yorkie, as with other terrier breeds, keeping the muscles and ligaments fit and strong helps to prevent patella luxation, which will be discussed further in chapter 12.

Being outside also benefits the bones, skin, and coat by exposure to sunshine, which provides vitamin D. Daylight also helps to regulate the sleep-wake cycle, as well as producing endorphins for emotional well-being, so it is important for your Yorkshire Terrier to spend time outdoors every day, even if the weather is not especially sunny. If it is cold or wet, however, the Yorkie may benefit from a jacket, as the breed lacks an undercoat and feels the cold more than most dogs.

As mentioned previously, outdoor exercise is also beneficial for socialization and training, as well as giving the Yorkie time to be a dog,

CHAPTER 3 Behavior

Photo Courtesy of Brooke Wells

exhibiting his natural behavior, whether that is chasing a squirrel up a tree or sniffing the trails left by rabbits, moles, and other dogs. In this way, the Yorkshire Terrier is exercising his busy mind just as much as his four legs.

Owners who are out and about with their Yorkies for much of the day may find that they have fulfilled the exercise requirement of their dogs without a dedicated walk; however, there is no substitute for some time in the park or countryside. The Yorkie should have at least one half-hour walk daily, which is less than many breeds, and may suit an older person; however, his need for exercise should not be overlooked, and if his owner is unable to fulfill this requirement for health or mobility reasons, then the help of a dog walker, privately or through a charity such as the Cinnamon Trust (UK) should be sought.

With a full understanding of the needs of the Yorkshire Terrier and a commitment to helping their dog learn to live harmoniously in a human environment, behavior issues may be effectively addressed, and a positive relationship established that will enrich the lives of both dog and owner.

CHAPTER 4
Preparations for a New Dog

Preparing Your Home

"I highly recommend setting up a small, quiet space in your home where your new Yorkie puppy can adapt to new faces, smells and sounds."

Jamie Sissel
Ashunee Yorkshire Terriers

If you have not owned a dog before, you may be wondering where to start in preparing your home for your new four-legged arrival. There are obviously things to buy, but let's start by making sure your home is safe for your Yorkshire Terrier and suited to the harmonious co-existence of dog and human.

Whenever you adopt a dog from a rescue shelter, you will be home checked. This is to make sure you live at the address you claim to, that you have thought about the implications of owning a dog, that the right dog is placed with you, and to flag up any alterations to your home that may need to be attended to before the dog arrives. The home check is not an exam or an interrogation, and is merely to facilitate a successful adoption and the safety of the dog. When you buy from a breeder, you may also be asked about the preparations you have in place for the dog, your lifestyle and working arrangements, how long the dog will be left alone, and your plans for the dog. These questions are because the breeder cares about the future welfare of the puppies. A vendor that lets their

HELPFUL TIP
Bringing Your New Yorkie Home

Like very young children, your puppy needs your protection. Begin "puppy proofing" before your new companion comes home. Yorkies will snoop about, so be proactive by removing household chemicals, electrical cords, and tempting indoor plants. Keep interior doors closed to avoid falling downstairs or entering rooms that are off-limits. Always err on the side of caution with a new puppy.

CHAPTER 4 Preparations for a New Dog

Photo Courtesy of Mike Voigts

puppies go without any checks or questions is not being responsible, so you should expect some kind of checks to be made at the initial stage of acquiring a dog and regard them as being in the best interests of the dog and you, the new owner.

Top of the list must be the security of your home. You may feel your home is very secure, and it may take the eye of an experienced home checker to spot a foxhole under the fence, or a broken fence panel. Maybe the fence does not quite extend to the far corner of the yard behind the shed, or in places it is low enough for a dog to jump over. Maybe your gate has a gap underneath that a small dog could squeeze through. Does your back gate have a lock as well as a latch? If you are considering a pedigree dog, which has a financial value, you should be aware that dogs can be stolen from unsecured back yards. They may also fall into the wrong hands if they escape. So, you need to ensure your back yard is completely secure at the outset, and continue to check daily for any breaches that may occur.

Remember, even if you already have a larger dog, there may be small escape routes that a Yorkshire Terrier could find, especially as they like to dig. So, it can help to adopt the mindset of a small dog when securing your back yard.

Be sure to clear any potential hazards in your back yard such as broken glass, and if you have a garden pond or swimming pool, this should be fenced off. Yorkies are not naturally drawn to water, but they are not the best swimmers if they should fall in accidentally.

If your house is on or near a busy road, you will need to ensure the dog cannot escape when you open your front door. If you have a front gate, it needs to be kept closed, with a sign to remind visitors to close the gate behind them. But you cannot rely on the compliance of others, so the dog should always be kept behind a stair gate or internal door when answering the front door, to ensure he does not bolt. This is a particular risk during the early months of owning a new dog, before he is accustomed to his home territory.

When preparing the inside of your home, you will have to make a decision from the outset as to which parts of the house the dog is allowed to access. There is no right or wrong answer to this, it is purely a matter of owner preference. However, if the dog is not allowed the run of the house, this needs to be consistent from the start. You may need to buy stair gates to shut off certain areas. Stair gates that can be opened and closed rather than stepped over will be a good investment since they will be permanently in place while the dog learns the rules.

If you have hard floors in your home, you are well prepared for the inevitable accidents a puppy will have, as well as any mud he brings into the home. If you have carpets, however, you may consider that now is not a good time to buy new ones. You may wish to restrict the dog to areas of the home that are not carpeted, or if your dog is to be allowed in your carpeted rooms, investing in a carpet vacuum/shampooer will certainly save the potential stress of accidental toileting in inappropriate places. Thorough cleaning to remove odors will also deter the dog from repeat soiling, and keep your home smelling fresh.

You may consider crating your dog at the puppy stage, to assist with housebreaking, to keep him contained at night and when you are out, and to give him a safe space that he can consider his place of security. Think about where to situate the crate. You will not need a large one for a Yorkshire Terrier, but a metal cage is always preferable to fabric mesh if your dog is to be left alone to prevent the dog chewing its way out.

CHAPTER 4 Preparations for a New Dog

Shopping List for Your New Dog

As well as a crate, which may be used for traveling as well as in the home, and a carpet shampooer, if you have carpets in your home, there are other things to buy for your new arrival. But the pet store is so overwhelming! The vast array of accessories available show how much we love our dogs and want to spoil them. But how much is really necessary?

The first thing you will need for your new dog is a collar and name tag. In some countries it is a legal requirement for a dog to wear an identity tag outside the home. In any case, it is a good idea. Your new dog should be microchipped, but if he should escape or stray, he may be immediately reunited with you if he is wearing an identity tag, which could save you a release fee if he otherwise ends up in the pound.

You will then need a leash. It is often possible to buy matching collar and leash combinations. Your dog, of course, will have no clue how coordinated his accessories may be, but it is part of the fun of dog ownership for many. In addition to a leash, it is advisable to get a harness for your Yorkie, for walking him near roads, as little dogs with small heads can easily back out of their collar, or the clasp may release; a harness is much more secure. It also saves the delicate bones of the neck from strain if the dog pulls or runs to the end of the leash.

Not everyone likes flexi-leashes, but they can give your dog more freedom walking in open spaces as long as they are used with a few precautions. Be aware that the lock on flexi-leashes may not always latch correctly and could fail with the result that your dog might run out in front of a car if he is being led on a flexi-leash near traffic. Short webbing leashes are recommended in town. Also, you should not let your dog be a nuisance by entangling himself in the legs of other people or the leashes of other dogs. When approached by other walkers, the leash needs to be retracted and the dog brought to heel. Used correctly, a flexi-leash can be useful to have until you are sure of your dog's recall.

Your dog obviously needs a bed. You do not need to go large. Dogs actually like size-appropriate beds, as they enjoy feeling cocooned by the sides of their bed. For a Yorkie, especially a miniature, even a cat bed will be plenty big enough. You may wish to buy more than one bed, so that your dog can settle in various parts of your home.

If you are not using a crate in your car, you will need a travel harness. It is an offense in some countries for a dog to travel unrestrained, and in any case, it is safest for your dog not to be thrown around in the event of an accident, or to cause one by ending up in the driver's footwell.

Photo Courtesy of Caitlin Morrell

You will need a bowl, or a couple of bowls for food. However, ordinary plates or saucers are perfectly adequate for a Yorkie. You will also need a water bowl, preferably earthenware with straight sides to prevent tipping.

You might consider a Kong or Nylabone to give your dog a distraction and something to chew on rather than the furniture. Rope toys and deer antlers are also popular. Avoid poorly made toys, especially with plastic eyes that may be swallowed or where the stuffing may come out and be ingested.

A pooper scooper may be useful for your garden, and you should consider where you plan to put the waste. You should also stock up on poop bags ready to clean up after your dog in public spaces.

Before buying food, you should check with the breeder or rescue what the dog is already being fed. Even if you have particular ideas on what you wish to feed your dog, changing over should be done gradually to avoid upsetting the dog's stomach, especially with the upheaval of a change in his living environment. Your dog may come with some of the food he is already being fed.

Likewise, do not go overboard with treats while your dog is adjusting. Treat him with his regular food in the early days.

If you are on a budget, do not feel pressurized by the list of things your dog may need. Most of these things do not need to be new. You may pick up secondhand items from yard sales, online auctions, or newspaper ads. Make sure you run all textile items through the washing machine to sanitize them and remove the smell of the previous owner, and thoroughly clean hard surfaces with sanitizer and soapy water. If you are creative, you may even make your own accessories such as bedding and nylon collars and leashes!

CHAPTER 4 Preparations for a New Dog

Introducing Your New Yorkshire Terrier to Your Other Dogs

"Make sure your Yorkie is vaccinated and is up to date on all shots before playing with other puppies its own age. With older or bigger dogs, make sure to keep a close eye on your puppy. A bite from a bigger dog can be devastating to your puppies welfare."

Elaine Schneider
High 'N Yorkies

If you already have a dog in your home, you need to accept that initially, he or she may not be as thrilled about the newcomer as you are.

If your dog is used to other canine visitors, such as friends' dogs, he will have no initial concept that your new dog is here to stay, and if the new dog is an adult, such as a rescue, there is little likelihood of fireworks at the introduction stage. The dogs may also gradually integrate and learn the hierarchy without too much bad feeling. However, bringing a new puppy into the home of an older dog is going to be a totally different dynamic. Puppies have very little experience of other dogs apart from their own mother and litter-mates. They have no social skills and cannot read the intent of other dogs. Your adult dog will regard the newcomer as impudent and in need of being put in its place, whereas the puppy may just want to play. Many a bad start has resulted in the new dog being returned, or even worse, the old dog being sent to a shelter. But the early days are no indication of the relationship that will develop given more time, patience, and careful supervision. Do not panic if your existing dog growls, snaps, and bares his teeth at the newcomer. It is part of establishing the ground rules and things will settle down. Be prepared for a settling in phase of up to four or five weeks, and during this time make sure you always supervise your dogs around each other, giving them scheduled separation opportunities for time out to relax; your adult dog may be especially in need of it.

Photo Courtesy of Elizabeth Nunley

Photo Courtesy of Lacy Spinelli

If you are adopting from a shelter, you may have had a "Meet and Greet" at the home check stage, and your existing dog may have already briefly met the newcomer. But now they need to acquaint themselves properly. Neutral territory is always best for first introductions, such as a park or neighbor's yard, so neither dog is feeling defensive. If the area is not enclosed, introductions should be on a loose leash, accompanied by a distraction such as a walk. If you do not have a neutral safe space away from your home, it is better for the dogs to meet outside in the yard than in the house. This introduction should ideally be off-leash if the yard is secure. Call the dogs apart every few minutes to ensure they do not get overexcited, and if you already have multiple dogs, introductions should take place one at a time. The first time you take the puppy indoors, the resident dog should be kept outside. Resident dogs are more accepting if they enter their house and the newcomer is already there rather than the new dog entering their space.

Remember your puppy is learning to interpret the language of your adult dog, and your adult dog is teaching the puppy to know his place, so you do not always need to intervene if things are looking heated. But you should be on hand in case your unsocialized Yorkshire Terrier puppy pushes things too far. He is a small dog that does not know his own size and could be a danger to himself if he is particularly provocative.

CHAPTER 4 Preparations for a New Dog

Introducing Your New Yorkshire Terrier to Children

If you have young children, you should talk to them about how to behave around your new dog at the preparation stage before the dog arrives in the home. Children are naturally exuberant, inquisitive and often careless. These endearing qualities may be less attractive to a new dog and could result in the child getting bitten or the dog getting teased, either of which could have lasting effects on the relationship.

Before your dog arrives, take your children to visit other child-friendly dogs owned by your friends, especially if any should own a Yorkshire Terrier. Teach your children that they need to be gentle around the dog. They should respect its space, allowing the dog to approach them or approaching the dog slowly and calmly, stroking the neck or back, rather than the face. Conditioning the child in advance of the arrival of the dog will not only facilitate a calm introduction, but also, if the child is fearful of dogs, they will have had a chance to meet some friendly dogs before one arrives in their home.

Once your new dog has arrived, involve your child in every aspect of his care. This not only teaches responsibility to your child from a young age, but it encourages the bond between your dog and your child. It also shows the dog that the child is above him in the hierarchy. Problems can arise if a dog tries to assert his dominance above the child in vying for top dog position. If your child is involved in feeding, training, and walking your dog with you, the dog will learn to respect your child. If you have children in the house, it is always advisable to ensure your dog does not become dominant, by disallowing him into your personal space on the furniture and particularly on the bed, where he may perceive he is top dog and consequently become defensive toward your children, seeing them as beneath himself and to be dominated. If this situation should arise you may consider consulting a behaviorist before it gets too engrained.

The good news is children tend to love Yorkies because they are small, non-threatening, and look like teddy bears. Yorkshire Terriers may have a reputation for being an old person's dog, grumpy and unfriendly, but this is not their natural inclination, and with respect, understanding, love, and discipline, they can be a great friend to your children, enabling them to grow up dog lovers themselves.

CHAPTER 5
How to Choose a Yorkshire Terrier

Purchasing or Rescuing?

So, you've decided on a Yorkshire Terrier. Good choice. Now you need to decide where to acquire your new canine companion. Purchased from a breeder, or rescued from a shelter?

If you want a puppy, you will usually need to purchase your dog from a breeder. Rescues generally offer older dogs, although not always. For example, a rescue may have a Yorkshire Terrier puppy that the owner has handed in because of a change of circumstances, or the puppy has proved more of a handful than they were anticipating. The worst time of year for bringing a new puppy into the house is Christmas, but puppies are often given as presents. It can soon become clear that this cute fluffball is in fact very demanding, messing in the house, chewing up the children's toys, yapping, and waking up in the middle of the night. These are transitory inconveniences, as any responsible prospective owner considering a puppy will anticipate, but all too often, as soon as Christmas is over, puppies will end up in rescue. The other occasion a shelter may have Yorkshire Terrier puppies is if a breeder has been shut down by animal welfare authorities and the dogs have been taken into rescue. So, if the idea of rescuing a dog in need appeals to you but you really want a puppy, it is worth looking online or phoning shelters to see if they have any Yorkie puppies looking for a good home.

One thing that will determine your decision to buy from a breeder is if you wish to show your dog at any level beyond fun local shows. In this case, you will need a puppy bred from Kennel Club registered parents. The Kennel Club in your country will have a list of approved breeders with puppies available, and if you have really done your homework, maybe attending dog shows, you may even recognize bloodlines that appeal to you. There is no denying you can expect to pay a premium for a Kennel Club registered Yorkshire Terrier puppy from champion bloodlines, but the pleasure of owning and showing an impressive example of the breed will certainly bring its own reward.

If you have any intention of breeding then you will need to select your bloodlines carefully, as the tight regulations put in place by the Kennel Clubs worldwide is to ensure the perpetuation of the best examples

CHAPTER 5 How to Choose a Yorkshire Terrier

of the breed. These, in theory, should have fewer health problems. A dog that is excessively inbred, however, should be avoided as certain genetic conditions are more likely to be apparent in such dogs.

However, you may not particularly want a puppy. This may be because you would prefer a dog that has grown out of the puppy stage, and may come with some training already in place. Or you may just feel there are too many unwanted dogs and you want to make a difference to the life of one of them. Or perhaps you are already an experienced owner, ready to take on a dog with behavioral or social issues from bad past experiences. In these cases, you may be looking for a rescue dog.

For many people, the satisfaction of turning a dog's life around by offering them a comfortable home and lots of love is what owning a dog is all about. Yorkies often find themselves in shelters because they have outlived their elderly owners. As we have already noted, Yorkshire Terriers are a long-lived breed, and are also popular with the older generation, so there may come a time in a Yorkie's life where he suffers a bereavement and needs a new human companion. Fortunately, Yorkies are adaptable dogs, and as long as their needs are met and understood, they will soon bond with a new owner. You should be aware, though, that a dog in its senior years may have age-related health issues that will need budgeting for. However, elderly Yorkies can continue to appear sprightly into their later teens. Some shelters may continue to fund medication for older dogs with existing health needs, but in these cases, they may offer a dog for fostering rather than adoption, to keep tighter control over monitoring the dog's health and welfare.

> **FUN FACT**
> **Purebred or Rescue?**
>
> Research is highly suggested before purchasing a purebred Yorkie. Do your homework. Investigate several breeders before purchasing your pet, and check online for reputable breeders at theyorkshireterrierclubofamerica.org. Be wary of "tea cup" varieties of Yorkies. Breeding for this one to three-pound variety is often done at the expense of the dog's health. A bright-eyed, energetic puppy will grow into a happy and lifelong companion.

Researching the Establishment

Photo Courtesy of Jodi Boerema

When buying a puppy from a breeder, it is important they should be registered with the Kennel Club in your country. This is because the Kennel Club works to ensure the best examples of the breed are allowed to perpetuate their genetics, for the health and welfare of the next generation. Whether or not you intend to show your dog, Kennel Club papers guarantee you have bought a dog with the best chance of growing up in good health.

The age of your puppy when the breeder releases him to you will usually be twelve weeks, by which time he will have started his vaccinations and been checked over by a veterinarian. The weight of a Yorkie puppy at twelve weeks is generally half his adult weight, so you will have a good measure of the size he is to grow to. Although the size of the parents may be an indication of this, in fact Yorkshire Terrier females can produce litters of considerable variation in size.

It is an extremely bad idea to buy a puppy from an unregulated breeder. In these instances, you may find yourself with a dog with genetic health issues, released too early from the mother, or that has not yet been vaccinated, in which case he may bring nasty diseases with him and not survive. You will also not have the necessary paperwork to show this dog, however impressive he may be.

High-quality show dogs that have been identified by the breeder at the puppy stage may be kept back until they are older before being released for sale, and in these cases, the breeder may only sell potential champions to experienced show dog owners who will fulfil the dog's show potential, and breed from their dog to perpetuate the bloodline.

CHAPTER 5 How to Choose a Yorkshire Terrier

Buying from a pet store has been outlawed in many countries, such as the United Kingdom. In countries where you can still buy a puppy from a pet store, you should consider this carefully. In encouraging this practice, you will be supporting a system that separates puppies from the mother too early and displays them in an environment that is not conducive to their well-being.

The term "puppy mill" comes with its own connotations of irresponsible breeding, and mass production of puppies for financial gain above welfare considerations. Such places are unregulated with dogs kept in cramped crates in unsanitary conditions. It is not possible to condone purchasing from an establishment of this nature; however, purchasers from puppy mills will often be unaware of the actual breeding conditions. They will be shown their dog in a clean room or area, far removed from its actual living environment. They will pay top dollar for a so-called pedigree dog with dubious papers; the parents, if shown, may not be the actual parents, and the dog may later be found to be in poor health with genetic faults. It is a guarantee of heartbreak and an animal welfare issue, so the purchaser should be astute in recognizing a puppy mill masquerading as a private breeder.

Rescue centers are the other alternative, but not all shelters are equal. The Kennel Club in your country will be able to recommend approved rescue organizations for the Yorkshire Terrier, although specialist breed shelters are in the minority, and most rescues take a variety of breeds, or specialize in small or large dogs. Some rescues may specialize in older dogs, or dogs with special needs. It is worth researching the shelters within your area carefully, as rogue rescues often pop up where the dogs may be kept in poor conditions or fostered out to unsuitable homes. These dogs clearly need rescuing from their misfortune in finding themselves in a poorly run so-called shelter, but they may bring a number of problems with them. The worst of these may be parvovirus if they have not been vaccinat-

Photo Courtesy of Stacey Bernier

ed. They may also have fleas, worms, skin conditions, matted fur, decayed teeth, or other unchecked veterinary conditions that will immediately drain your finances, and may lead to further health struggles. A responsible shelter, on the other hand, will attend to all veterinary needs, and advise on anything that needs to be followed up. The dog will be chipped and vaccinated, and will come with a guarantee that if circumstances change, the shelter will always take the dog back.

Rescuing a dog does not mean it will be free. Responsible shelters have invested financially in the dogs they take in. The rehoming fee goes some way toward covering veterinary care, neutering, vaccination, microchipping, and administration. It also ensures dogs are not taken for dubious purposes such as dog fighting. You can expect that any responsible shelter will carry out a home check to ensure your suitability for the dog you are interested in, and will try as far as possible to match you with the right dog. It is unfair for a rescue dog to experience further upheaval in its life by being placed in a new home that is not going to work out.

Inquire about Parents

If you are adopting a rescue dog, you are unlikely to know anything about the dog's background. In fact, even if a rescue takes a dog with pedigree papers, it will not usually pass these on, to ensure the dog is taken for the right reasons and for anonymity regarding the previous owners. Therefore, you are taking some chances with the dog, but if he is reasonably healthy it is a calculated risk.

If you are buying a puppy, however, there are some important questions to ask. Firstly, you should ask the vendor if they bred the puppies themselves, and ask to meet the mother and father of the puppies. A refusal to this reasonable request should flag a potential issue. You should inquire as to the ages of the mother and father (the mother should be over one year old but not more than seven), and whether they have had any health issues. Check that the mother has had no more than three litters in her lifetime. Ask to see the pedigrees of the parents, and look for excessive inbreeding, where the same names appear on both the mother's and father's pedigrees, or on different branches of the individual pedigrees. Inbreeding may produce dogs with genetic problems.

CHAPTER 5 How to Choose a Yorkshire Terrier

Photo Courtesy of Sydney Upton

Looking at the Puppy

Most breeders will release their puppies at twelve weeks, although a puppy may leave its mother at eight weeks after weaning. If the puppy is obviously not weaned you may question whether he is as old as the breeder claims. You should check that the puppy looks healthy, with clean eyes, ears, and bottom, and has not been recently bathed to disguise a problem. He should be bright and inquisitive. You will probably make an instinctive connection with an individual puppy in the litter, but don't let your heart rule your head. Do make these basic checks, and take your new puppy to a vet for a full check-up as soon as you take him home. If the vet spots any problems, a responsible breeder should take the puppy back at this stage without question.

Photo Courtesy of Yesayi Kirakosyan

Behavioral and Health Considerations with a Rescue Dog

Some of the reasons a dog may find itself in rescue have already been discussed. He may have been seized along with others from an illegal puppy mill, he may have outlived his owner, his owner may have had a change of circumstances or not have had the foresight to anticipate the demands of dog ownership. Not all of these situations will have caused psychological damage to the dog, but even in the best cases, the dog will have experienced upheaval, and been removed from its human with whom he may have formed an attachment. Dogs are very loyal and can bond even with a person who mistreats them. If the dog has been severely mistreated, however, he may come with considerable psychological and behavioral issues. Any responsible rescue will not place such dogs with inexperienced owners. If, however, you do find you have rescued a dog that has more baggage than anticipated, you should contact the shelter for support. They may be able to offer their experience to help you address the dog's problems, or put you in touch with an approved behaviorist.

The rescue wants every adoption to work out. It is not helpful to the dog's state of mind to return to rescue, or to go through many changes of ownership, and if you are committed to the dog and want to make it work, it is the rescue's responsibility to support you. Ultimately, every responsible rescue will take back a dog if the rehoming does not work out. That is the guarantee they make to take care of the dog's future, and why you never actually own a rescue dog, you adopt instead.

When a shelter takes a dog, they will have it checked over by a veterinarian, so any health issues will be identified and treated or notified to the adopter. Unneutered dogs will be castrated or spayed to prevent unwanted breeding and for the benefit of their future health. The dog may be treated for fleas, worms, and skin conditions, will be brought up to date with its vaccinations, and may have a dental procedure. So, your rescue dog comes with a full service. The rescue may even cover any existing health problem. It is always advisable to take out veterinary insurance as soon as you acquire the dog, and before it presents with any further health issues, as these would be exempted from cover if the policy is not taken out until after first presentation of any condition.

Whether buying a puppy or offering a rescue dog a home, careful selection will ensure the perfect partnership, and a friendship for life.

CHAPTER 6
Training

"Yorkies are small and need frequent potty breaks. We have found the crate training method has worked well. Once they wake up from napping, the first step is to take them outside immediately and reward when finished, let them have playtime in a small area and after play take another potty break, again reward. It takes consistency."

Jamie Sissel
Ashunee Yorkshire Terriers

It is vitally important to the welfare of your dog that it is trained. Previous chapters have mentioned—and hopefully debunked—the myth that the Yorkshire Terrier is untrainable. It has been demonstrated that Yorkies are actually capable of a high level of training, but not every owner wishes to teach their dog to walk a tightrope, neither are such stunts especially condoned if a dog is still permitted to be a dog. However, a compromise needs to be found between the Yorkshire Terrier's natural animal instincts, and its suitability to share the home and life of its human.

> **HELPFUL TIP**
> **Happy Trails**
>
> Traveling with your Yorkie should start early. Sometimes, dogs associate car outings with going to the vet's office or grooming. Short trips in the car will get your dog accustomed to the activity. If you plan on taking your dog out of the country, check with the airline about accommodations. Look to see what is required in the country you're entering. Vaccination documents, license information, and proper tags should be updated and handy while traveling. Don't forget to have a microchip placed in your dog.

The instinctive ability to learn is evident in the case of Pavlov's dog, where the experimental scientist Ivan Pavlov famously noticed that his canine subjects would salivate when presented with food. He then introduced a specific sound at meal times, and found that even when food was not present, the dogs would still salivate at the sound, demonstrating that a dog can form associations in the brain, a useful process termed "classical conditioning."

Over the years, different training methods have fallen in and out of favor. Early dog training methods were often harsh and punitive, when a dog had a job to do and a no-nonsense working relationship was more important than an emotional connection. Some harsh methods persist today, but as animal psychology has gained ground and dogs have increasingly become companion animals, more humane methods have become popular, focusing on positive reinforcement rather than punishment.

Today, there is a wide range of dog training methods, and it is testament to the dog's adaptability that any of these may yield results. However, it is important that the owner is consistent with whichever training method they choose to follow, otherwise their Yorkie will become confused and training will be frustrated. Therefore, although some simple suggestions to teach basic commands are given in this chapter, if you are attending classes with your dog, you should continue with the training method that is being taught. All training takes patience, and if results seem slow in coming, they will be achieved with persistence and consistent application. Chopping and changing training methods if instant results are not achieved will be counterproductive.

The other important thing to bear in mind is that training needs to be practiced on a daily basis, whether attending classes or not. If the owner goes to a class with their dog once a week, they need to be practicing the commands for the six days in between. If the owner prefers not to attend a class, they need the self-discipline to practice training on their own initiative. The early months with your Yorkshire Terrier may seem like hard work, but it will be worth it for the reward of living many years with a well-trained dog.

Although Yorkies are not especially food-orientated like some breeds, they can still be highly motivated by a delicious training treat. Equip yourself for training with small, pungent treats that your dog cannot resist, such as tiny pieces of cooked sausage or bacon, or tiny dried liver treats that you can make yourself by drying cooked liver chips for four hours in a very low temperature oven or in a dehydrator. Training treats can also be purchased in pet stores, or you can cut soft meaty strips into tiny pieces. Remember to adjust your dog's feed ration accordingly, but his main food should always be his nutritionally balanced kibble.

Toilet Training

It goes without saying that if a dog is to live in the home, he can't be allowed to toilet inside the house, as to do so creates an unhygienic and unpleasant living environment. Therefore, as soon as a puppy is able to control his bladder and bowels, he should be trained to toilet outside.

It is natural for a dog not to soil his own sleeping area, so if you are crate training your Yorkshire Terrier, you are already at an advantage with toilet training. In these instances, your Yorkie will instinctively be holding his bladder and bowels in the crate, and will be ready to find release when he is taken out of the crate. By taking him outside and praising him at the point he urinates or defecates, you have been able to anticipate the desired action and can associate it with a command. This command should be a short word of your choosing, such as "Busy," "Potty," Wee-wees," or the like, and said purposefully as soon as you see your dog squat or start to raise its leg. Just like Pavlov's dog, your Yorkie will eventually associate the word with the desired action, and urinate on command.

If you are not crate training your dog, he should be taken outside frequently, and the command word only used when he is visibly beginning to relieve himself, otherwise the association will be meaningless.

CHAPTER 6 Training

If you are clicker-training, then at the point of a positive result, you can click and treat your dog. If you are not clicker-training, a small treat will reinforce the point that he has done good work. Praise and attention are always welcomed as your dog really wants to please you, and will repeat the positive behavior when he understands it is what is required of him.

With young puppies who have limited bladder control, paper training can be an introduction to toilet training, as a puppy will be drawn to an absorbent surface such as newspaper or a puppy pad if he feels the urge to relieve himself before the owner takes him outside. This paper can be gradually made smaller and moved toward the back door and then outside. Once your dog is relieving himself outside, the command and treat method may be taught.

If your dog should soil in the house, it is important to understand that he should not be chastised after the event, as he will not know why you are reprimanding him. Only if he is caught in the act of relieving himself indoors should the command "No!" be used, whereupon he should be taken outside to learn the association of where is the appropriate place to relieve himself.

The other thing to note is that soiled areas in the home should be cleaned with a special pet cleaner, as household cleaners containing ammonia smell of urine to a dog and simply reinforce the idea that toileting should happen in the same spot. For the same reason, it is important to neutralize the natural smell of urine, as apart from being unpleasant to live with, it tells your dog that it has permission to toilet where this has already occurred.

If you have a male dog, toilet training may be complicated by the dog's instinct to mark its territory, creating urine scents around the home. It is always recommended that male dogs be castrated to reduce this unwanted behavior.

You may find that your Yorkshire Terrier is not at all keen to go outside to do his business in wet weather, as Yorkies really can be especially wimpy when it is raining. In challenging weather conditions, you may have to enforce the point by putting a coat on him and taking him around the block on a leash, where he may sniff a scent and instinctively cover it. Or you may provide a newspaper by the back door in situations where you can't win the battle, so that you don't lose the war. This compromise keeps the owner's upper hand without setting back toilet training, with less stress to both owner and dog.

How to Teach Sit

When teaching commands to your Yorkshire Terrier, the first thing you need to achieve is your dog's full attention. From the early days of ownership, the Yorkie should begin to recognize his name, after which the first command to teach your Yorkie is "Look at me." To do this, sit your dog facing you in a room with no other distractions. With your index finger point to your eye and as the dog makes eye contact, say purposefully, "Look at me." If the dog remains focused, reward him with praise, or click and treat if you are clicker-training.

After achieving eye contact with the "Look at me" command, it is time to teach your Yorkie to sit. As the Yorkshire Terrier is a small dog, this should be done from a crouching or kneeling position as your dog will find it difficult to maintain eye contact when you are standing. With a treat in one hand, bring this hand to the dog's nose and back over the head of the dog toward its tail. Its head will rise to follow the treat as you do this and instinctively its hind quarters will lower to a sitting position. This may be gently encouraged with the other hand. As the hind quarters lower, say the command "Sit." The dog needs to learn the command in association with the action, so until he has learned the command word it should not be used to tell the dog what to do, but to tell the dog what it is actually doing.

It can be useful to have a hand signal to go alongside the sit command, and this is an outstretched arm with the palm uppermost. The arm should then be bent so the hand comes up to the shoulder. This upward motion has a similar instinctive effect on the dog to cause them to lower the hind quarters.

When the dog has achieved the sit, remember to praise him, and if you are using a treat to give it as a reward. Then repeat the exercise several times. It should become more immediate each time.

How to Teach Stay

Once your dog understands to focus on you with the command "Look at me" and then to sit, you can teach him to stay.

With the dog in the sit position, stand up and stretch out your arm with your palm facing the dog. This puts a psychological barrier between you. Use the command "Stay" at this point, as he has not yet moved, so he is effectively staying. Step back from the dog, maintaining eye contact. If he is still staying, use the "Stay" command again. Then return to the dog, praise and reward.

Photo Courtesy of Lucas Abner

The next step is to move further away incrementally, and eventually to turn your back on the dog and walk away, releasing eye contact in the expectation that the dog will still remain seated in the same spot.

If your dog gets up and follows you, do not use the "Stay" command while he is not actually staying, but when you have put him back on the spot and it is focused again for the next attempt.

Once your dog is a pro at sit and stay in an indoor environment, practice outdoors where there are more distractions, but always within an enclosed area unless you are using a long training leash for the dog's own safety.

How to Teach Lie Down

By the time you get to the "Lie down" command, your Yorkie will have gotten the idea that by learning what you want he will earn your praise, and will be very ready to show how clever he is. Eye contact should be second nature to him at this point as he eagerly awaits the next instruction.

With your dog in the sit position, you now want him to lower his chest and front legs to lie down. You can use the command "Down" or "Lie down" for this, but it is important not to use the same command when your dog jumps up without permission or it will create confusion. "Off" is the command for this.

With your dog's attention on you, and a treat in one hand, bring this hand to the dog's nose and then low to the floor in front of him. Then move the treat away from him toward yourself. His natural instinct is to follow this movement, causing him to lower his chest and creep his legs forward in the direction of the lying down position. As the dog lowers its body into the correct position, use the command "Lie down," praise and treat. Repeat until the action is instinctive.

CHAPTER 6 Training

How to Teach to Walk on the Leash

Even though the Yorkshire Terrier is small, he may still be naturally inclined to tow his owner with surprising strength when out and about if not taught to walk nicely on the leash.

In days past, a choke chain was commonly used to teach a dog to walk on the leash without pulling; however, this harsh training aid is rarely used now and should not be considered for a Yorkshire Terrier as it could cause real damage to the delicate skin and neck anatomy on a small dog. It is advisable to use a harness on a Yorkie, as even though stronger dogs may abuse a harness by leaning into it, it diverts the tension to the chest that is better equipped to take the strain than the neck. Also, the small head of a Yorkie may easily slip its collar, so a harness is safer when being led outside of the home.

Walking on the leash needs to be taught intentionally with positive reinforcement just like the other commands, so begin in a distraction-free environment. With the dog on your left, walk forward with some small treats in your hand to give while the dog is walking to heel. As soon as the dog runs ahead, stop walking. When he stops at the end of the leash, walk on, but only keep walking while the leash is slack, and treat the dog while he is walking by your side.

The command "Heel" can be used when your Yorkshire Terrier is walking nicely alongside you. Once he has learned the association, the command can be used to bring him back to heel when he pulls on the leash.

Be aware that patience is needed in training your Yorkie to walk nicely to heel, and walks can take considerably longer, or be considerably shorter in length than you planned, but the end results will be well worth the effort.

How to Teach to Walk off the Leash/Recall

Being able to trust your dog to come back means that he can enjoy the freedom of being walked off the leash in safe spaces. While you are teaching recall, it is important that the dog is in an enclosed area, or you use a lightweight long training leash for his own safety.

When you first let your Yorkshire Terrier off the leash, you should release the clip when the leash is slack, not while the dog is pulling, so that the dog is let off on your terms and not on his own. Using positive and engaging words of encouragement, get the dog's attention by calling his name and the command "Come" at frequent intervals during his

Photo Courtesy of Anthony Fiallo

first short time off the leash, being a fun person to be with and provider of attention and treats. Change direction so the dog has to keep sight of you. Never chastise the dog for coming back just because he ignored you the first time, as he needs to learn coming back gets rewarded, not punished. He also needs to know coming back does not mean going home, so call him back, treat him, and send him away again frequently during the training process.

Again, timing is important for word association, so the command "Come" should be used initially when your dog is heading toward you, so that it can be rewarded as the correct response. Only when the dog has learned the word and what it requires should "Come" be used to call the dog back from its alternative plans.

Remember, Yorkies are highly driven by small prey animals, and will lose all sense of reality if a squirrel crosses their path, so until your dog has good recall, care should be taken not to put your dog in situations where he may forget himself in pursuit of a fast-moving target. Open spaces are preferable to woodland for off-leash walks, and enclosed parks are a safer option for your dog.

CHAPTER 6 Training

Agility

Owners and dogs that really enjoy obedience training and wish to take it to the next level could consider agility classes as a fun way to exercise their dog and strengthen the bond between them. Although agility is dominated by the brilliance of Border Collies, all breeds can participate at their own level, and classes will be grouped accordingly.

Agility training can start from 9 months but 12 months is usually preferred, so that the puppy has developed sufficiently. In the case of the Yorkshire Terrier, poles may not be used at all to start with, and then set low as due to their size jumping may damage growing muscles and bones. But there are plenty of other agility obstacles to navigate, such as weaves and ramps that are perfectly within the capabilities of the Yorkshire Terrier, and if it is something that he enjoys, it is a great way of having fun and improving obedience training.

To sum up, when training your Yorkshire Terrier, it is important to:

1. Expect the best! Your dog is capable of learning and wants to please.
2. Tune in to your dog—understand his mind and anticipate his actions.
3. Keep it simple, at least to start with.
4. Be consistent—choose a training method you can stick to.
5. Be patient and persistent—training takes time.
6. Reward your dog when he gets it right—he really wants to!
7. Make it fun!

CHAPTER 7
Traveling

"Yorkies love adventure. They want to be where their family is. Our Yorkies travel in a small Sherpa bag and take in all the new sounds and smells while looking out the window."

Jamie Sissel
Ashunee Yorkshire Terriers

Taking your dog on vacation with you can be an exciting experience. You may also need to travel with your dog on a day-to-day basis, such as to the park or to the vet. There are lots of options for how to travel with your dog. Dogs can travel well in cars when trained from a young age, and you can often travel with your dog in an aircraft too.

Sometimes your dog will have to stay behind though. In that case, there are several options available to ensure your dog is cared for how you wish. In this chapter we will explore all the options of how to take your dog with you, and also what to do if you can't.

Preparations for Travel

If you are going on an extended trip, it is a good idea to have a health check with your veterinarian first. This way, if any vaccinations have lapsed or are going to lapse soon, they can be boosted. These vaccinations should be recorded in a vaccination record booklet, which is important to take with you when you travel. The veterinarian can also give some worming and flea treatment to take with you as well as a repeat prescription of any chronic medication to make sure you have enough until you get back from the trip. If you are traveling internationally, your dog might require a health certificate and exportation paperwork, which the veterinarian can provide at this time.

Hopefully, while you are away, your dog will not need to see a veterinarian. It is a good idea, however, to do some research about where you are going and be prepared for an emergency. Find the phone number of the closest veterinary practice and save it in your cell phone alongside the number of your regular veterinarian, so that if you need to visit a vet

CHAPTER 7 Traveling

Photo Courtesy of Jamie Pokropski

in an emergency, you can easily provide the contact details of your usual veterinarian. That way, any relevant clinical records can be shared between them easily.

All dogs should have some form of identification on them, but it is especially important when going away, as the dog will not be familiar with the area if he gets lost. Make sure your leash and collar are sturdy, and the collar has an identification tag on it, detailing your name and number. Some people like to have a second tag when traveling with details of the address and phone number of your vacation spot; however, this is not essential. Having a microchip inserted is also very useful, as a dog can break out of a collar, but a microchip is permanent. Remember to keep your contact details up to date with the microchip company, as an old cell number registered to the microchip will render it useless.

Traveling in a Car

Many dogs tolerate traveling in a car very well, but it is worth getting him used to being in it before traveling. Let him sit in it with you on the driveway, and practice small drives before going on a long one.

A dog can safely travel in a car by several different methods. Most owners find a crate is the most convenient way to transport a dog in a car. The same crate can be used in the house as a doggy den or to sleep in at night, and therefore the dog may come to find it to be somewhat of a familiar sanctuary for him. The crate should be large enough to allow the dog to stand up, turn around, and lie down without touching the sides. It should be made of strong materials with handles on the outside, and no protrusions on the inside where the dog could get hurt. All four sides should have some form of ventilation, such as a meshing, and placed in the car so that fresh air can easily flow into the crate.

Some owners do not like crates, and would prefer the dog to be a bit freer. Fitting a dog guard above the back seats will enable a dog to be loose in the trunk of the car, without the danger of him trying to jump over the back of the seats. Dogs should never be loose in the open bed of a truck, as this is extremely dangerous.

Dog seatbelt harnesses can also be bought which are an excellent alternative to keeping your dog in a crate or in the trunk. They are arguably the safest way for a dog to travel in a car, as if the car is in a crash, then they will not be thrown about. However, the dog will have to sit on the back seat of the car, which for some people is a deal breaker, especially if they have an expensive car or need all the seat space for passengers.

Some dogs get carsick when they travel in a car. This doesn't necessarily mean they will vomit though. Sometimes they may just drool whilst traveling or be reluctant to get in the car if they remember being nauseous from the last time they traveled. Carsickness can be overcome by traveling when your dog has an empty stomach, if it is a short drive, or requesting some travel-sickness tablets from the vet to give your dog half an hour before the journey, if it is a longer drive.

Traveling can be boring for everyone, including your dog, so make sure you have some of his favorite toys packed in with him. Also make sure any children sitting on back seats do not entertain themselves by taunting the dog during the trip, as this can make the trip very stressful for your dog.

When you travel, ensure that everything for the dog is packed and easy to access. Dogs should be offered water at least every four hours

CHAPTER 7 Traveling

Photo Courtesy of Sierra Draucker

and food at least every 12 hours, so having easy access to plenty of food and water is vital. It is also important to frequently stop to allow your dog to exercise and relieve themselves. When you stop, never leave your dog in the vehicle unattended, particularly if it is hot. Dogs can quickly die in hot cars.

If you are traveling by car in hot weather, keep the car cool by turning on the air conditioning. If you do not have air conditioning, open the windows but only a few inches and ensure your dog is secured. You should never allow your dog to hang out of the open window of a moving car. Car sunshades will also keep your dog out of direct sunlight, and you may need to stop more often for the dog to drink if you do not have air conditioning.

Traveling by Plane

When traveling internationally by plane, it is important to contact your veterinarian several months before the trip to understand what must be in place for allowing your dog to cross the border. Different countries will have different requirements, and it is the owner's responsibility to make sure everything is in place. Most airlines will require a certification of health from a veterinarian, no older than 10 days before travel, and possibly a passport or other exportation paperwork. Rabies vaccinations must be up to date, and vaccination certificates will need to be presented when traveling. Some countries will also require a blood test three months prior to travel to prove that the rabies vaccination has been effective.

Dogs cannot travel if they are less than eight weeks old, and for some destinations, they require the dog to be at least 12 weeks old. Each airline will have variations on their services, so inquiring about these when you make the reservation is important. Some dogs may be allowed in the cabin with you in a crate, while other airlines will only allow the dog to go as hold luggage in a crate.

Federal regulations do not allow live animals to be hold baggage or cargo if the animal will be exposed to temperatures below 45 degrees Fahrenheit or above 85 degrees Fahrenheit during departure and arrival, and during connections. If the destination may be outside of this temperature range, some exceptions may be made on presentation of a veterinary certificate stating that the dog is used to these conditions, and that they will not be subject to these temperatures for more than four hours.

CHAPTER 7 Traveling

Vacation Lodging

Make sure you find out in advance that the accommodations you wish to stay in allows dogs. Many will not, and some may have size or number restrictions. However, if they are a dog-friendly place, do remember that not all guests and staff will be comfortable with a dog. Therefore, it is important to respect other people nearby. Try to keep your dog as quiet as possible, and do not leave him unattended as he may bark or destroy the property since he is alone in an unfamiliar place.

Photo Courtesy of Chelsea Chapman

When arriving, ask the management staff where you can walk your dog and make sure you pick up any mess he makes on the walk. In the end, it should only take a normal cleaning of the room by the staff to make it appear that no dog has been there.

Leaving Your Dog at Home

Sometimes it is not possible to take your dog with you on vacation, which means that he will have to stay at home. There are several different options to ensure he gets the best care possible while you are away. These options should be thoroughly researched to make sure you are leaving your dog in capable hands.

Friends and Family

Some people will choose to take their dogs to friends or family to be looked after while they are away. This is a good option if they are dog-savvy people and it allows you to know exactly who is looking after your dog. Also, the dog will be familiar with them too, which reduces stress all around.

Often, friends or family will be doing this as a favor, so it is important to remember not to impose too much. Make sure you provide them

HELPFUL TIP
Patience is a Virtue

Indoor vs. outdoors? Yorkies can be trained to relieve themselves on puppy pads or in a lined litter pan. Of course, going outside for a nice walk is always best, although not always trouble-free. Your Yorkie may have a strong opinion on the weather, snow and rain especially. When you house-train your Yorkie, be patient. Some owners train Yorkies for agility competitions or as therapy dogs. Training of any kind will take time and a calm, positive approach. Investing time into training your Yorkie will reap many benefits.

with enough food for your dog to last the entire vacation, as well as vital equipment such as a collar, leash, dog bowls, crate (if used at night or in the car), and toys.

If they have their own dogs, this might provide a good opportunity for entertainment for your dog; however, these dogs may not be happy for another to come into their territory. Before leaving your dog, make sure the other dog is happy with having another dog around in the house and does not get defensive or stressed.

Before leaving your dog, ensure that you friend's garden is appropriately dog-proofed, as even if they have their own dog, it does not mean that there aren't any holes under the fence. A larger dog may not be able to get out of a Yorkshire Terrier–sized hole, and a dog in its home environment may also not be as inclined to try to escape.

Kennels

Kennels can be a convenient option; however, different kennels will operate at different standards. Make sure you visit the kennels several times before your trip to ensure that the standards are consistent with your expectations.

At a kennel, dogs will usually be placed in a structure where there is an outdoor run, and an indoor shelter with a bed. These are cleaned out several times per day, and will be where food and water are offered. Dogs are taken out once daily for a walk or a communal area playtime with other dogs, to make sure they get plenty of exercise.

The downside to placing your dog in kennels is that they won't receive as much one-on-one human attention that they are used to. For some dogs, this won't matter and they will cope very well, but for others, they may become stressed or bored.

Before placing your dog in kennels, talk to your vet to make sure they are up to date with their vaccinations, especially against kennel cough. This can be very easily picked up in areas where there are high densities of dogs. Some kennels will not allow dogs to use their facilities without up-to-date vaccination records, so it is important to inquire about their requirements before booking.

House Sitters

Hiring a house sitter is becoming increasingly popular, and is an excellent way of ensuring your dog is looked after in their own environment. House sitters come and live in your house while you are away, and look after your pet as if they were their own. They also provide excellent security for your house, as it will not look empty while you are gone.

There are many credible house-sitting companies, so reading up on their past reviews is a good way of finding someone who is suitable. They should be clean and neat people, easily contactable, and have plenty of experience with pets. It will be a bonus if they provide daily updates on your pets while you are away.

Before traveling, invite the house sitter on a walk or over to the house for the afternoon, so that your dog can meet them and bond before you leave.

This is not the cheapest option if you need to leave your dog behind, but you can rest assured that they will receive excellent professional care.

Regardless of how you travel and whether or not you decide to take your dog with you, a vacation should be a fun experience. A calm owner will help keep their pet calm. Pets are very perceptive to our stress, so prepare in advance for any long journeys or pet sitting services, so that you can be relaxed and confident that all will go to plan.

CHAPTER 8
Nutrition

Importance of Nutrition

Without a healthy diet, it is impossible for you to have a healthy animal. Food is a daily aspect of a dog's life, so special attention to it should be paid. Many owners, breeders, and even veterinarians are not knowledgeable about the best nutrition for dogs, and the only reliable source of information is directly from a veterinary nutritionist or scientific journals. However, this chapter will outline what sort of nutrition is best for your Yorkshire Terrier, what diets are available, and how to assess the quality of a diet when confronted with numerous choices on the shelf of a pet store.

Photo Courtesy of Sophie Thackray

CHAPTER 8   Nutrition

Commercial Food

"Always feel a high quality kibble. Do your research and know the ingredients in your Yorkie's diet. If you choose to cook for your Yorkie, it's best to give a daily supplement or use kibble as a treat. Or you can always mix a little kibble into the cooked meal provided."

Marsha
Miracle Yorkies

There are many choices of food to choose from for your Yorkie, and knowing exactly which one to choose is impossible for someone without any nutrition knowledge. Many people will have personal opinions on foods which have or haven't worked for their dogs; however, every dog is an individual, and therefore it is important to remember even if the food hasn't suited the neighbor's dog, it doesn't mean it won't suit yours.

Dry or Wet

Commercial pet foods normally come in a choice of dry or wet preparations. Dry foods are condensed, so for a dog to ingest the same amount of nutrients, far less dry food is needed in comparison to wet food. You can test if a dry kibble is of good quality by adding half a cup of water to half a cup of dry food, and leave for half an hour. If it expands to twice its initial size or more, it means that the dry food is full of bulking agents and will possibly make the dog feel bloated and full. If it only expands a little, then it is of a higher quality and better for the dog.

Dry food can come in a variety of kibble sizes. For Yorkshire Terriers, a small kibble size is the most appropriate. Dry foods with small kibble pieces are usually branded on the packaging as "small breed" or "toy breed." Some dog food companies have foods on the market specifically for Yorkshire Terriers, which are usually based on a small kibble size and added ingredients for a healthy, glossy coat.

Dry food is better than wet food for dental health, as by crunching through the biscuits, plaque is removed from the outside of the teeth. This will reduce dental disease and gum inflammation as the dog gets older.

Wet food, in comparison to dry food, is far more palatable. Dogs with dental disease, or puppies who do not have strong jaw muscles yet, may prefer eating wet food due to the ease of chewing it. Yorkshire Terriers are notoriously picky eaters and are usually more enticed by wet food, to the detriment of their teeth.

> **HELPFUL TIP**
> **Finding the Sweet Spot**
>
> Consult your dog's veterinarian regarding your Yorkie's nutritional needs. A 6-12- week old puppy should be fed small amounts four times per day. A puppy at three to six months of age can be fed three times per day, in quantities recommended by your vet. Between 6-12 months, twice a day feedings are advised. After age one year, split the required daily food allowance into two feedings, morning and night. Remember, feeding your Yorkie at regular times will assist with house-training. Take the dog outside to relieve itself 10-20 minutes after eating. "Watch the dog, not the dish" is sage advice when it comes to feeding amounts.

Puppy Food

All puppies should be started on a commercial puppy food when obtained from the breeder. Puppy foods will state "puppy" or "junior" on the packaging. These foods are the most appropriate for their growing bodies, as they are higher in protein, calcium, and phosphorus than adult foods.

AAFCO Standards

All commercial pet foods in the USA must meet the Association of American Feed Control Officials (AAFCO) standards. These are nutritional standards set out by the AAFCO which detail the concentrations of nutrients, minerals, and vitamins. There are two main categories: adult and growth phases. These standards ensure that any dog food which meets these standards will be well balanced and not detrimental to your dog in any way.

BARF and Homemade Diets

The general public is becoming increasingly health conscious, eco-friendly, and concerned about the sources of ingredients. By creating your own food for your dog, it allows you to make sure that all ingredients are locally sourced, natural, organic, and wholesome. It sounds idyllic; unfortunately, however, it is often to the detriment of your dog.

Homemade diets, whether they be cooked diets or bones and raw food (BARF), are usually very poorly balanced and can contribute to health issues such as brittle bones, stunted growth, bladder stones, and internal ill health. It is strongly advised that either a veterinary nutritionist creates these recipes if homemade diets are strongly desired, or alternatively pre-balanced, frozen handmade meals are purchased from a manufacturer.

These meals which have been prepared by a manufacturer, especially if they contain raw foods, will usually have been balanced with additional minerals and vitamins, as well as tested for toxins and microbes.

CHAPTER 8   Nutrition

Microbes in BARF diets are a cause for concern. Raw food can contain high levels of Salmonella, E. coli and Campylobacter, which can be passed easily onto humans through the dog licking their coat or drooling on their owners. Therefore, if a dog is being fed a BARF diet, household hygiene precautions must be very strict, especially with vulnerable people such as children and the elderly.

Pet Food Labels

A lot can be deciphered from a pet food label, which gives an insight into the quality of the food. All pet food labels must contain an ingredients list, which is usually in order of weight, and a guaranteed analysis, which details the protein, fiber, moisture, and fat content of the food.

Guaranteed Analysis

The guaranteed analysis cannot be compared for wet and dry dog foods, as the percentages given are on an "as fed" basis, and therefore some calculations must first be done to directly compare them.

The percentage of the nutrient of interest must be divided by the percentage of food which is dry so that they can be compared. For example:

A wet food with a moisture content of 75% will therefore be 25% dry. If the protein content is 5%, the calculation will be 5/0.25 = 20% protein on a dry matter basis.

A dry food with a moisture content of 10% will therefore be 90% dry. If the protein content is 20%, the calculation will be 20/0.9 = 22.2% protein on a dry matter basis.

Once the dry matter basis has been calculated, the guaranteed analysis is an excellent source of information for protein, fat, and fiber. Often, it will also include carbohydrate and ash information. These details need to be taken into consideration alongside the ingredients.

Photo Courtesy of Laura Ruckel

Ingredients

Photo Courtesy of Kenn Donahue

A high-quality food will have a meat protein source as its main ingredient. There should be lower quantities of starch-based filler ingredients in comparison to protein-rich meat ingredients.

It is important to understand that meals, for example chicken meal, which are dehydrated, ground meat, contain almost 300% more protein per gram compared to the fresh meat that they are derived from, and so since they are light in weight, they will be further down the ingredients list than if the manufacturer had used the fresh meat.

Meats used in dog foods are usually beef, lamb, salmon, or chicken, and just because the packaging states it is chicken flavor, it doesn't mean the only meat in it will be chicken. If a dog suffers from a food allergy, it is usually these common meats which are the cause. Changing to a more novel protein source, such as venison, duck, turkey, or tuna, will often alleviate some of the symptoms.

Fish proteins are excellent sources of omega-3 and omega-6 fatty acids. These are excellent for ensuring the health of the coat, skin, brain, and joints. In the correct ratio, they can also have anti-inflammatory effects, which will help reduce the discomfort associated with allergic inflamed skin and arthritic joints.

Common vegetables in dog food include peas, carrots, sweet potatoes, and potatoes. These are full of minerals (potassium, iron, and magnesium) and vitamins (mainly vitamins A, B, and C) to help keep the dog healthy.

CHAPTER 8 Nutrition

Potassium is a vital mineral which helps keep the heart beating regularly and also is involved in the conduction of signals along nerves up to the brain. Iron is used in the formation of red blood cells which transport oxygen around the body. Magnesium helps maintain strong bones and teeth. Vitamin A contributes to the health of the eyes and nervous system. Vitamin B is found in several different forms, and plays a role in cell metabolism. And finally, vitamin C helps improve the immune system to successfully combat infections.

Grains, such as rice, barley, and oatmeal, are also regularly found in dog foods. These can be cheap to source and are commonly used as starchy fillers. They are high in fiber, which is excellent for the health of the digestive system as they regulate how much water should be in the guts. If the dog has loose stools, the fiber will stimulate the body to absorb some of the water from the guts into the blood. Likewise, if the dog is struggling with hard stools, it stimulates the body to draw water into the guts to soften them.

Some dogs are sensitive to grains in the diet, though, either causing digestive upsets or itchy skin. There is minimal scientific evidence behind grain sensitivities; however, the anecdotal evidence of their effects is extensive.

Weight Monitoring

Maintaining a good weight is important for the health of your dog. The Yorkshire Terrier is a breed which is prone to weight extremes. Since picky eating is a characteristic of the breed, some Yorkshire Terriers may stay in a natural state of being underweight. On the other hand, due to the size of Yorkshire Terriers, many owners do not realize their exercise requirements, and the dogs then can easily become overweight.

Being overweight poses a major danger to your dog as he ages. Firstly, any excess fat is naturally stored in the liver; however, when too much fat accumulates in the liver, it is put under extreme stress. The liver has many vital roles in the body. It produces bile which aids in digestion, it filters out toxins and drugs in the body, and finally, it plays an important role in metabolism of proteins. If it is not working efficiently due to fat buildup, then all these systems will be affected.

An increased weight long term may also lead to your dog developing diabetes. When the body has to constantly work hard to decrease the blood sugar level by producing large amounts of insulin from the pancreas, it starts to either become resistant to the insulin or it begins

Photo Courtesy of Yesayi Kirakosyan

to struggle to create the insulin. As a result, your dog then cannot control the blood sugar levels, which can lead to increased thirst, increased urination, lethargy, vomiting, and an effect on the appetite. Once he has developed diabetes, he will have to be treated with twice daily injections to bring down the blood sugar levels.

To avoid health problems associated being over- or underweight, putting your dog on the scales is not the best way to monitor it. Every dog is an individual, and one Yorkie might be overweight at 6 pounds, whereas another might be perfectly healthy at 12 pounds.

The most scientifically proven method of monitoring the weight of a dog is by using a body condition score (BCS). This is a scale of 1 to 9 in dogs and cats (not to be confused with a scale of 1 to 5 in horses and farm animals). The ideal weight is a body condition score of 5. The scoring is as follows:

BCS 1 = Extremely underweight. Ribs, lumbar vertebrae, pelvic bones, and bony prominences are visible from a distance. Major loss of muscles and no obvious body fat.

BCS 3 = Underweight. Ribs easily felt and may just be visible. Not much fat present. Obvious waist and obviously tucked up abdomen. Some visible bony prominences. Tops of lumbar vertebrae easily seen.

BCS 5 = Ideal weight. Ribs easily felt with minimal fat covering. Waist can be seen when standing behind the dog. Ribs just visible when looking from above the dog. Abdomen tucked up when viewed from the side.

CHAPTER 8   Nutrition

BCS 7 = Overweight. Heavy fat cover over ribs and difficult to feel. Noticeable fat deposits in lumbar region of back and base of tail. Difficulty viewing waist. Slight abdominal tuck.

BCS 9 = Obese. Very large fat deposits over base of tail, spine, and chest. No waist or abdominal tuck. Distended abdomen. Fat deposits around neck and limbs.

Yorkshire Terriers, due to their extensive coats, may be slightly harder to body condition score than most other breeds. It is best to rely on touch more than sight to body condition score Yorkshire Terriers. It is easy to assume a dog is at a healthy weight with a large coat, but when it is felt, it could be very skinny. Another way to stop the coat from hindering body condition scoring is to wet it down.

Ensuring your Yorkie maintains a healthy diet and weight will be beneficial to both him and you, as you will be providing your dog with the best chance of a healthy, long lifetime.

CHAPTER 9
Dental Care

Importance of Dental Care

While the Yorkshire Terrier is generally a hardy little dog, its teeth are one of its downfalls. Like many other small-breed dogs, dental disease is a common occurrence and most owners will have to make decisions regarding dental interventions at some point in their Yorkie's life. Therefore, it is imperative that you take a positive stance against dental disease from when you first acquire your dog, and make a conscious effort to prevent the deterioration of his teeth throughout his lifetime.

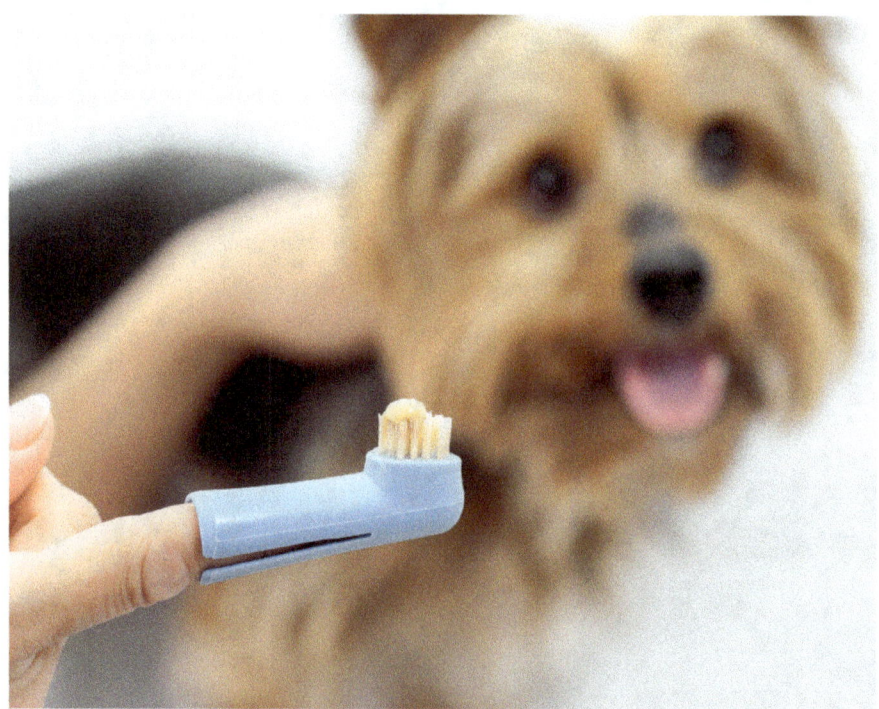

CHAPTER 9   Dental Care

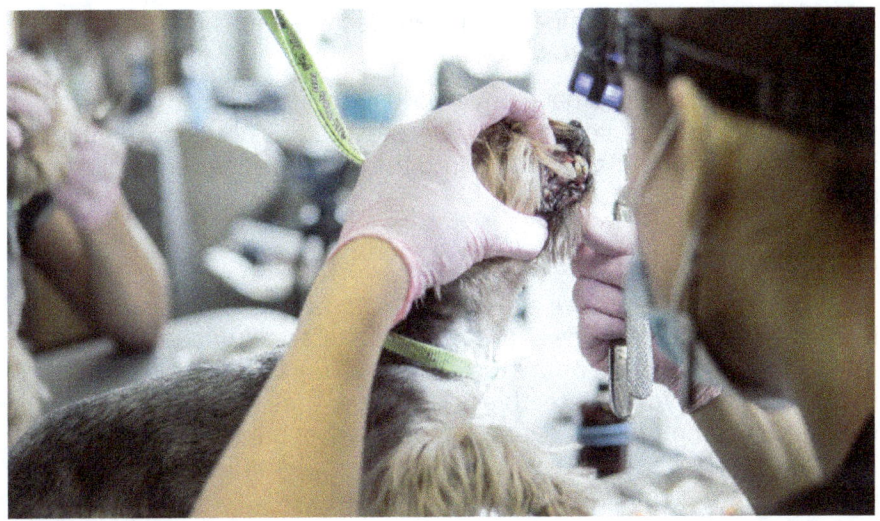

Dental Anatomy

The tooth is a bony structure which sits in a socket of the maxilla (upper jaw) or mandible (lower jaw). Dogs have 42 adult teeth, but initially start off with 28 deciduous (baby) teeth. A tooth is like an iceberg, where only a small portion of it is visible. The visible portion is called the crown, and the portion which sits in the socket is called the root. The tooth is held in the socket by periodontal ligaments, which are extremely strong. The outside of the tooth is covered in a protective layer called enamel. Finally, the center of the tooth has a fleshy area called the pulp where numerous nerves reside, hence why tooth pain is so uncomfortable.

Breed-Specific Dental Issues

Residual Deciduous Teeth

Before the adult teeth come through at roughly one year of age, the mouth is full of baby teeth, known as deciduous teeth. As the adult teeth begin to erupt, they are supposed to push the deciduous teeth out of their socket. Most owners will never notice their dogs' teeth come out as they will be lost or swallowed, but for the Yorkshire Terrier, sometimes they won't come out at all.

When the adult tooth erupts next to the deciduous tooth, the mouth becomes clustered with unnecessary teeth. While this usually doesn't cause much pain for the dog, the deciduous tooth must be removed, as food can easily become impacted in between the teeth and lead to decay and permanent damage to the adult tooth.

Most owners opt to have any residual deciduous teeth removed at the time of neutering, so that only one anesthetic is needed. The deciduous teeth only have shallow roots into the gum, making removal a quick and simple procedure.

Clustered Adult Teeth

Yorkshire Terriers have extremely small mouths to fit all their teeth in. Some Yorkies therefore end up with clustered adult teeth, especially the incisors at the front, or the molars at the very back. The incisors sit in shallow sockets, so if the teeth are clustered, they may fall out easily. It is not an uncommon sight to see a gappy Yorkie, but even though it may look unusual, if the teeth have just fallen out due to clustering, it is of no detriment to the Yorkie.

Gingivitis and Plaque

Gingivitis is the term used for describing inflammation to the gums. This is usually in response to plaque buildup. Yorkshire Terriers are a breed that suffers with excessive plaque on their teeth, which tends to aggregate on the base of the tooth, around the tooth-gum junction.

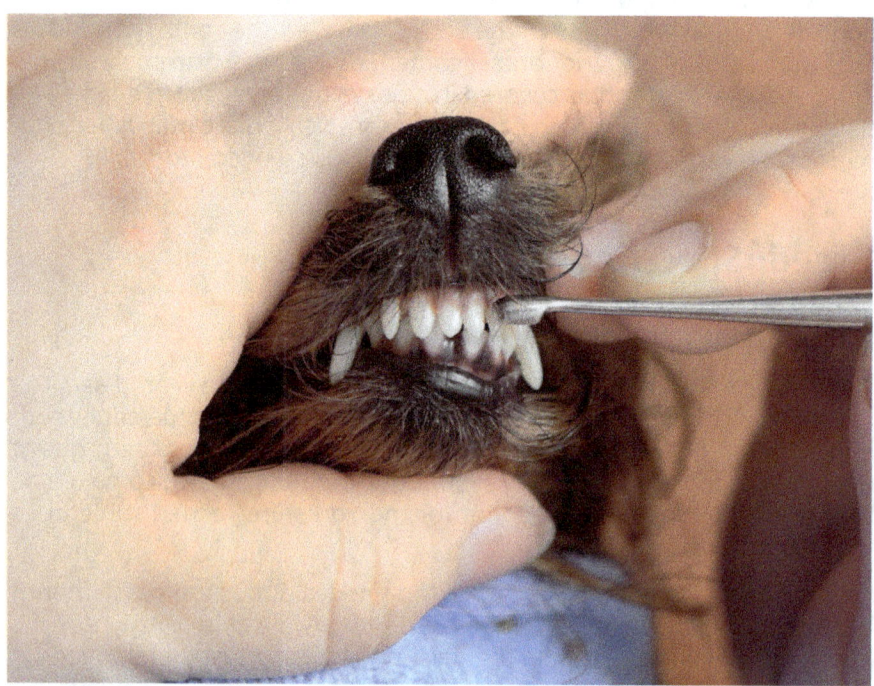

CHAPTER 9   Dental Care

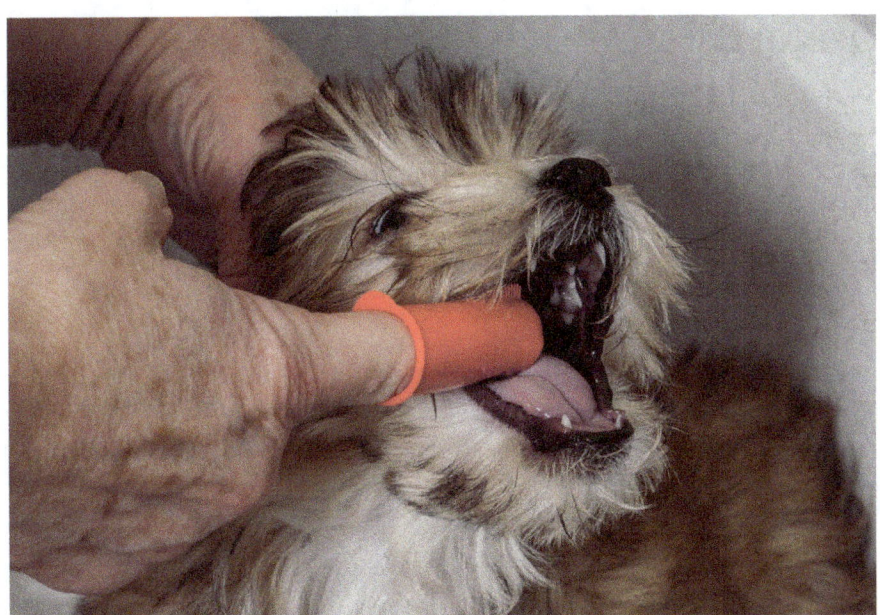

Plaque is a buildup of excess food material and bacteria, and can be smelly and foul tasting to the dog. This is the main cause of bad breath. When plaque is in contact with the gums, the body sends white blood cells to the area to fight the bacteria, but this in turn causes inflammation in the gums. Yorkshire Terriers tend to accumulate more plaque than other breeds, and as a result, their gums become very inflamed and painful.

Premature Tooth Loss

Yorkshire Terriers are prone to premature loss of their adult teeth. Most dogs only start losing their teeth when their age reaches double figures, if they lose their teeth at all; however, Yorkies may start losing adult teeth as young as five years old.

Tooth loss is mainly attributed to chronic inflammation of the gums, as this will weaken the periodontal ligament which holds the tooth in the socket.

Dogs can eat food very successfully with very few teeth, so this should not be a worry for the owner, but the process of losing a tooth can be uncomfortable for several months during the period that the tooth is wobbly, so it is important to try to avoid tooth loss all together. A dog happily eating is not a sign that there is no dental disease. Many dogs will continue to eat despite their mouth being uncomfortable.

Dental Care

Dogs do not naturally accept routine dental care, unless they have been trained to perceive it as a positive experience. It is prudent to start dental care from a puppy so they learn that it is part of everyday life, and make it a fun experience with lots of playtime and positive interactions afterward. Dental care can take many forms; examining, brushing, treats, and mouthwash.

Examining

**HELPFUL TIP
Safeguarding Your Dog's Health**

Every breed is susceptible to particular health concerns. Because Yorkies have overcrowded mouths with 42-45 teeth, they are known to have dental problems. They are prone to tooth decay, plaque and tartar buildup, gum disease, and infection. Since they are vulnerable to dental problems, owners are advised to begin brushing their puppy's teeth daily. It is important to have dental cleanings every two years or as advised by your veterinarian.

Examining the mouth for plaque buildup should be done on a monthly basis. Some dogs do not tolerate owners or veterinarians looking in their mouths, but this is usually because they are not used to it.

To examine the teeth, firstly lift up the front lips to look at the incisors. Plaque, which is a gray or brown sticky buildup at the gum line, decay, tooth discoloration, or redness of the gums should be noted.

Next, the corner of the cheek should be pulled far back to examine the premolars and molars for the same issues on both sides.

Finally, the mouth should be opened wide from the front, to look on the inside of the teeth.

Some veterinarians will also feel the submandibular lymph nodes during their dental check. These are two spherical structures around the area of the curve of the jaw. If the lymph nodes are enlarged, it usually means they are reactive to bacteria in the mouth. These are not usually routinely felt by owners, and require training to learn what is normal or abnormal.

Brushing

Brushing the teeth should be done at least every other day. Many owners neglect brushing their dog's teeth, but if the effort is put in to brush them just for one minute, several times per week for their whole lives, it has been proven to significantly reduce the risk of dental disease later in life.

Brushing should be done with a toothpaste specifically for dogs. They are usually poultry or beef flavored and contain enzymes which aid in dissolving the plaque off the teeth. Human toothpaste should never be used. The foaming agent in human toothpaste can cause liver damage to dogs, and if xylitol has been added, which is a sugar-free sweetener, this can cause the dog's blood glucose to drop dangerously low.

For dogs who have not been trained to have their teeth brushed from a young age, and do not tolerate it well, simply smearing the toothpaste on the teeth several times a week will be significantly more beneficial than doing nothing at all.

Brushing can be carried out with either a dog toothbrush or a finger brush. Dog toothbrushes come in a variety of sizes and understandably, the Yorkie needs the smallest size available. Ensure that all teeth are brushed, especially the back teeth which are often missed, both on the inside and the outside.

Treats

There are many dental treats on the market which can be bought to aid dental health. The premise behind them it that they cause friction to the outside of the tooth, thereby removing plaque buildup.

When selecting a dental treat for a Yorkie, a small-breed dog chew is the most appropriate. One-size-fits-all-type chews will be less effective, as your Yorkie may not be able to get his mouth around it in an appropriate way, and therefore not bite down effectively enough for the chew to do its work.

Some people prefer more natural dental treats, rather than manufactured treats. Knuckle bones are not advised, even though chewing them will aid in scraping off the plaque, as they are prone to splintering or pieces breaking off, which if ingested, can cause blockages or damage to the intestine.

A good alternative to knuckle bones are deer antlers. These are usually sourced from ethical culling operations, and while they can be pricey, they last a very long time. Deer antlers do not splinter or break into pieces, and dogs enjoy gnawing on the projections. They usually are cut up into different sized pieces. The best piece to choose for a Yorkie would be on the smaller side, but not small enough for it to be eaten whole if there are larger dogs within the household as well. The antler should be discarded before it has been gnawed down small enough to be swallowed.

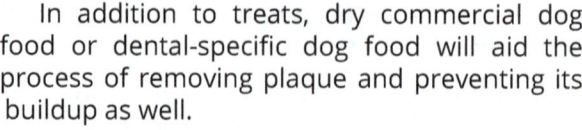

In addition to treats, dry commercial dog food or dental-specific dog food will aid the process of removing plaque and preventing its buildup as well.

It is important to remember that any additional calories which are given in the form of treats should be compensated for when considering how much food a dog should have when fed their meals.

Mouthwash

Like human toothpaste, dogs must never consume human mouthwash either. However, there are mouthwash-style products which can be used to help fight plaque in dogs. These liquid products are usually added in small volumes to drinking water, and work on the same premise as dog toothpaste; they are filled full of enzymes which aid in dissolving the plaque off the teeth or stop more plaque from forming.

Dental Procedures

Dental care should be adhered to on a regular basis for Yorkshire Terriers, since they are prone to so many dental problems. If it is not, most Yorkies will need to have a dental procedure during their lifetime.

Dental procedures are carried out by veterinarians under general anesthetic. Usually the procedure will only require a day visit to the vet. A general anesthetic will be required because sharp tools and scalers will be in the mouth of the dog; therefore, it would be impossible and dangerous if the dog was in a state where he could move. The dog will need to be brought to the vet in the morning having not had any food, to avoid any vomiting during the anesthetic.

The veterinarian will start by examining all the teeth with a probe to understand which ones are loose or have pockets into the socket where the periodontal ligament is no longer effective. These will be marked for extraction at a later part of the procedure.

Next, he will use a scaler to remove all plaque from the outside of the teeth. The scaler squirts water during the scaling process so that the teeth

CHAPTER 9   Dental Care

do not warm up too much from the friction, and that all plaque is washed out the mouth. Scaling the teeth will leave them pearly white like a puppy again.

Now that all the bacteria have been removed in the plaque, any teeth that need to be extracted can be taken out. This is only done after scaling because if the mouth is full of bacteria, then bacteria can be embedded deeper in the gumline during the extraction process, which in turn can cause nasty oral infections. The extraction process can be tricky if some of the tooth is still firmly attached to the periodontal ligament. A sharp tool, called an elevator, is slowly run around the tooth root to weaken the ligament until it is wobbly enough to be pulled out.

If the tooth has left a large socket, the veterinarian may choose to flush out the socket and then stitch it closed. Not all veterinarians do this, due to the worry of stitching in a deep infection; however, if the mouth is sufficiently flushed, then the benefits may outweigh the risks. The healing time is significantly shortened by stitching closed, and if it is stitched closed, then no food will get stuck in the pocket when the dog eats.

Finally, the teeth are polished with an abrasive paste to ensure they are as clean as they possibly can be. This paste usually has a nice flavor to it and aids in freshening the breath of the dog.

Even though having a dental procedure may seem stressful to both you and your Yorkshire Terrier, the long-term benefits massively outweigh the stress. Dental disease is not pleasant, and your dog experiencing it is likely to have toothache and a constant foul taste in his mouth. By routine home dental care, and a dental procedure later in life if needed, his mouth can stay as clean and pain-free as possible, leading to a happy dog and happy you.

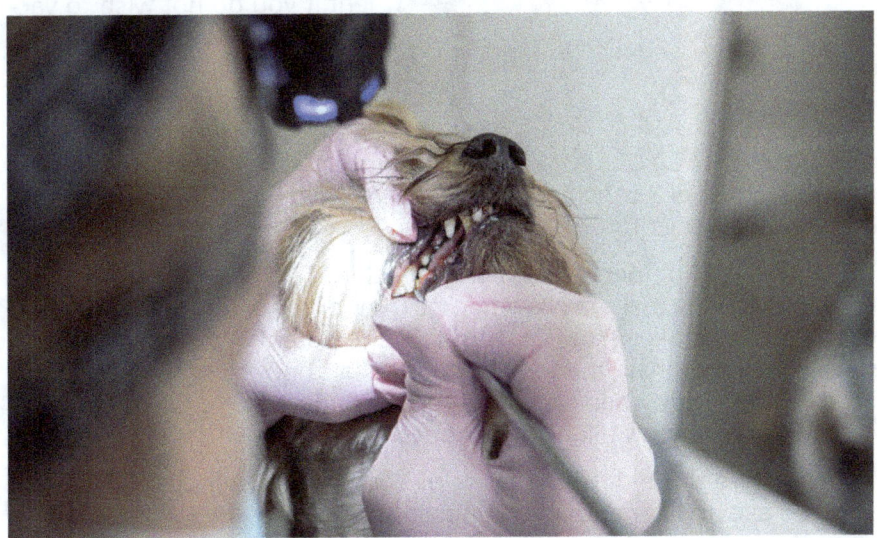

CHAPTER 10
Grooming

"If you choose to keep your Yorkie's hair long, you will have to comb it daily. The best comb is a metal comb with rotating teeth. Make sure the tips of the teeth are soft and not sharp. If you decide to keep your Yorkie's hair short, the grooming is minimal, but you will have to take him/her to the groomer about every 4 to 6 weeks."

Marsha
Miracle Yorkies

About the Coat

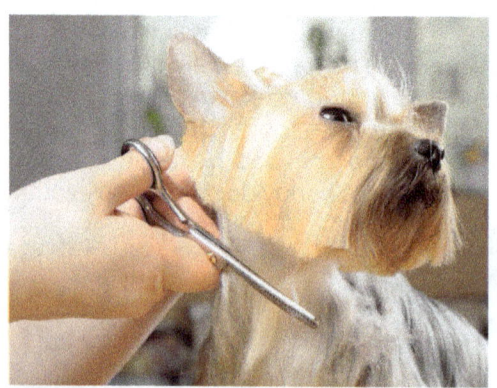

One of the main attractions of the Yorkshire Terrier is its coat. The coat is non-shedding, with the exception of the occasional loose strand of fur, which is excellent if you do not wish to vacuum on a daily basis. In addition, Yorkshire Terriers have extremely little dander (flakes of skin) in their coat, in comparison to other breeds, and therefore they are considered a hypoallergenic breed for people who are allergic to dogs.

Different from most breeds, the Yorkshire Terrier is also single-coated, which means there is not a thicker layer of fur underneath the main coat. While this allows the coat to have the potential to grow long and sleek like human hair, it does also mean that they are prone to becoming cold, especially when wet. Therefore, it is advisable to purchase a dog coat for them when walking in wet or cold weather.

There are three different types of Yorkshire Terrier coat, which depend on age and genetics of the individual:

CHAPTER 10 Grooming

Puppy Coat

The puppy coat is thicker and softer than the adult coat. It often is also a different color; usually black and tan. As the dog gets older, the coat usually fades in color. This puppy coat can last up to 24 months.

Silk Coat

The silk coat is the standard set by the American Kennel Club for Yorkshire Terriers in the show ring. It is long, sleek, and shiny, and hangs straight all the way to the floor.

Wavy Coat

The wavy coat is more textured than the silk coat and rarely grows more than a few inches. This coat can give a cute, scruffy appearance to the Yorkshire Terrier. Unfortunately, this coat is harder to manage than the silk coat as it becomes matted if not regularly brushed.

Coat Health

The health of the coat is largely influenced by the health of the dog. If the dog is receiving excellent nutrition, has no external parasites, such as fleas, and no allergies or underlying diseases, the coat should be of a good quality.

To improve the coat further, you can add omega 3 and omega 6 supplements to your dog's diet. Some diets already have these added, and they are naturally high in concentration in fish-based diets. Omega oil supplements, formulated for dogs, are widely available on the internet and through pet and vet stores.

To keep your Yorkshire Terrier's coat well maintained, brushing and bathing is required. Most people in the general dog-owning population, however, tend to over-bathe their dogs. Shampooing too often can strip the coat of its natural oils, which leads to the coat becoming dry. A dog does not need to be shampooed more regularly than once every six weeks, and for many dogs, two or three times a year is perfectly fine. If they become muddy or dirty in between these shampooing sessions, rinsing down with warm water will clean the coat sufficiently without stripping out the natural oils.

There are many different types of shampoo on the market, and for dogs without skin allergies, most of them will be acceptable to use.

CHAPTER 10   Grooming

However, if your dog is prone to sensitive skin, then tea tree or oatmeal-based shampoos are best, as they will soothe the skin as well as clean the coat well.

Unlike shampooing, brushing should be done on a regular basis for optimal coat health. The type of coat the Yorkshire Terrier has will dictate the grooming method to use. Two types of brush are needed; a slicker brush, which contains fine wire bristles, and a greyhound comb, which is a metal comb with different spaced bristles at each end.

When grooming a wavy coat Yorkshire Terrier, the coat must first be inspected for mats. These are common under the armpits, in the groin area, around the ears, and around the neck. These can be sensitive to brushing and are best cut or shaved out. Next, gently brush through the coat with a slicker brush, not going over the same area more than 3 times as the bristles can be sharp and cause irritation to the skin. Once the coat has been brushed with the slicker brush, go through the whole coat with a greyhound comb to find any mats or tangles deep in the fur that you might have missed.

The silk-coated Yorkshire Terrier requires a different grooming technique. The best method is known as the "line grooming method." This is where the hair is parted so that the skin can be seen in a line, usually parallel to the ground along the length of the body. The hair below the line is then combed gently with a greyhound comb until it is knot-free, and then the hair is parted a little higher up, and it is all repeated again. This is to be continued until you have groomed the whole coat.

If desired, professional groomers can bathe, wash, and trim the coat for you on a routine basis. Some groomers will come to your home, while others have a dedicated grooming salon. The groomer will expect your dog to stand still on a table to be brushed and trimmed, and therefore it is advised to introduce the dog to the groomer from a young age so they are aware of what is expected of them.

> **FUN FACT**
> **"A Little Off the Top"**
>
> How much time and money do you want to spend on grooming your Yorkie? There are dozens of "haircuts" available to choose from, but you may want to do some research first. Hop online at yorkieinfocenter.com/yorkie-hair-cuts to see options for your dog's grooming needs. If you are unsure what style will fit your needs and wallet, discuss options with your groomer. Don't be afraid to bring a picture to share your ideas. Be specific. Whether your dog's coat is short, medium, or long make sure you are thorough when dropping off your dog at the groomer's office. Once you find a groomer you trust, request her/him each time you schedule your routine every six to eight-week grooming.

External Parasites

It is important that the coat is kept free from parasites such as fleas, ticks, mites, and lice. These can be contracted from other animals, and not necessarily just dogs. A routine anti-parasite treatment should be administered to kill off any parasites in the coat or on the skin, as well to provide a long-lasting protection from the parasites.

Anti-parasite treatment can come in several forms. The most common is a pipette which is emptied onto parted hair, directly onto the skin, on the back of the neck. Other options for treatments include collars, treats, injections, shampoos, and pills. The best course of treatment should be advised by a vet, and administered as frequently as the product label displays.

It is imperative that dog treatment is not given to cats, and likewise cat treatment is not given to dogs, as in the best-case scenario, it will not be suitably effective. In the worst-case scenario, the product could kill the animal.

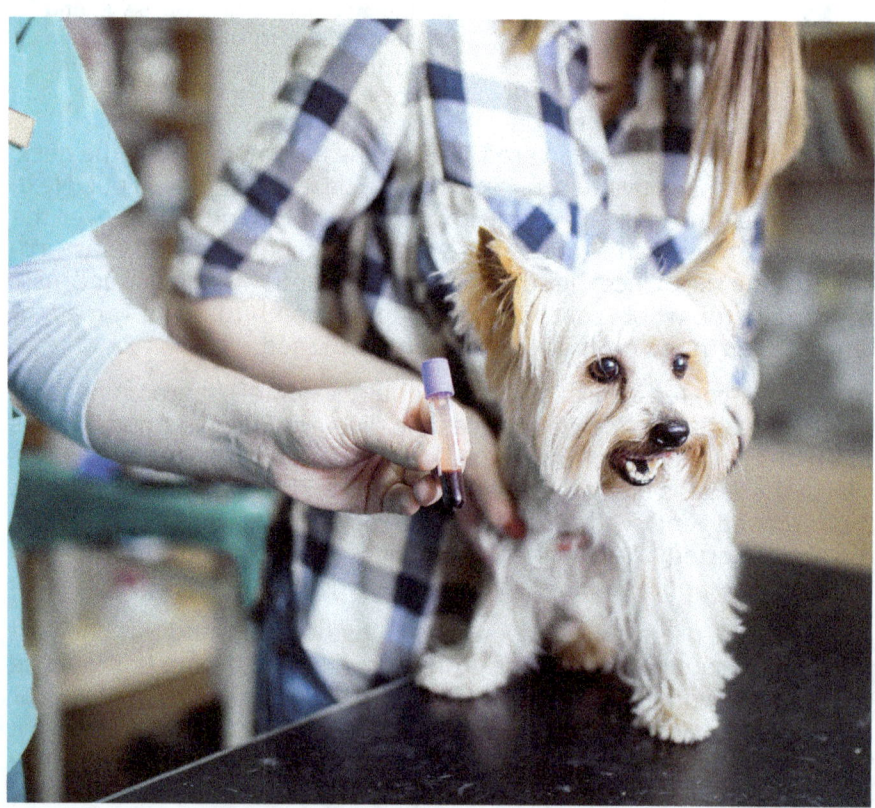

Nail Clipping

As part of the grooming process, your dog's nails must be regularly monitored and clipped when necessary. The timeframe will differ from dog to dog, and will be impacted by the frequency of walking on hard and abrasive surfaces, which act as nail files.

It is imperative that the nails are continually monitored, as due to the curved nature of the nails, if they are allowed to grow too long, they could curve around and imbed in the pads underneath the paw. This not only is extremely painful, but can lead to infection and open wounds, which are difficult to treat as the pads are slow healing areas of the body.

In the average dog, the nails will need to be clipped roughly every 1–2 months, but you should be continuously monitoring them.

The dog has five nails per front leg, four on the paw, and one dewclaw on the inside of the leg, and four nails per back leg, all on the paw. Some dogs have a recessive gene which causes dewclaws to be present on the back legs too.

Each nail is made up of keratin, and folds around a fleshy center called the quick. For most dogs, the keratin does not completely meet underneath the nail, which makes clipping them a little easier as explained later.

To clip the nails, you can purchase a dog nail clipper of an appropriate size for the nail. These can be purchased from any pet store, and also from many vets and supermarkets. When clipping the nails, it is important to judge where the quick might end. It is full of blood vessels and nerves, and if cut, it will not only cause the dog a considerable amount of pain, but it will also bleed profusely. For dogs with unpigmented nails, it can easily be seen through the keratin. For dogs with black nails, the easiest way to judge where the quick ends is to turn the paw upside down, as often it can be seen in the gap where the keratin does not quite meet. If it is accidentally cut in the process, the most ideal method is to stem the bleeding with a silver nitrate cautery pen, which can also be bought from pet stores. Failing that, applying firm pressure for 5 minutes with some cotton wool or a cloth will also be successful.

Many dog owners are nervous about cutting their own dogs' nails, especially when the dog is wriggly or has had a bad experience in the past. If that is the case, it is best that the nails are cut by a veterinary nurse or a professional groomer on a frequent basis.

Ear Cleaning

Ear cleaning is something that is not necessarily needed on a routine basis for Yorkshire Terriers. However, there are some specific scenarios whereby it is important that the ears are not neglected.

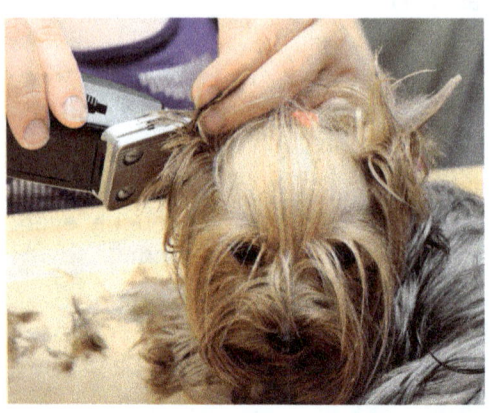

Many professional groomers will pluck the ears of Yorkshire Terriers as they grow hair inside their vertical ear canal. It is a common belief that this hair can be the cause of ear infections as it traps dust and external debris. On the contrary, the hair is present to stop debris from accumulating further down in the ear canal and therefore prevents ear infections. Unfortunately, when a groomer plucks the hair from the ear, it leaves the sensitive ear lining red and inflamed, which results in a weaker barrier against bacteria, yeasts, and ear mites, leading to potentially more ear infections.

You should clean your dog's ears with a canine ear cleaner on a regular basis, as prescribed by the veterinarian, if he suffers from intermittent or chronic ear infections. Also, if he enjoys swimming or getting wet on a regular basis, they should be cleaned after each time. If this is not the case, the ears only need to be cleaned once or twice a year.

The best ear cleaners you can buy can be purchased from a veterinary practice, pet shop, or online. It should be of a slightly acidic pH (6.5) and clearly state on it that it is for dissolving or removing wax and debris from the ear canal. The slightly acidic pH creates an environment within the ear which discourages the growth of bacteria and yeast.

The method of cleaning is very simple, but often messy. First the flap (pinna) of the ear is lifted and the nozzle of the cleaner is placed in the entrance to the ear canal. Gently squeeze the bottle and then place the flap of the ear over to block any cleaner from leaking out. The flap of the ear can then be massaged for 30 seconds. When the flap is lifted up again, your dog should be allowed to shake. This will bring all the separated debris out from deep inside the ear. Finally, wipe the debris away with some cotton wool.

Anal Glands

For most dogs who are being provided with enough fiber in their diet, the anal glands rarely cause an issue. But for dogs who do not have enough fiber, who regularly have loose stools, or have abnormally positioned anal glands, the anal glands will frequently fill up. This is uncomfortable for the dog and the dog will scoot or rub his bottom along the floor to try to relieve them.

Anal glands are two small sacs, each side of the anus, positioned in the four and eight o'clock positions. When they become filled, if they are not emptied of the fecal material, an abscess can easily form and burst. This can lead to a draining tract through the skin which heals very slowly. Recurrent infections might indicate that the anal glands need to be surgically removed, which is a risky surgery as the nerves which influence the tone and control of the anus run very closely to the anal glands. If surgery is indicated, some owners opt to remove one anal gland at a time to lessen this risk.

Anal glands should be emptied by a trained professional such as a veterinarian, veterinary nurse, or professional groomer. Most groomers routinely check and empty anal glands as part of their service, but it is not necessary to routinely check them if they are not causing any issues.

If your dog is constantly having repeat issues with the anal glands, increased fiber can be added to his diet through changing brand to a food with a higher concentration, or by adding a fiber supplement to the food. Fiber will increase the firmness of the stools, which in turn squeeze the anal glands as a stool is passed, emptying them naturally.

CHAPTER 11
Preventative Veterinary Medicine

Choosing a Veterinarian

Choosing a veterinarian is an important consideration when you acquire a new dog. While many owners jump from vet to vet, there are major benefits in having some continuity. If the vet knows your dog well, then they are familiar with their history of health care and diseases.

When choosing a veterinarian, there are several factors to consider as outlined below.

Finances

Veterinarians are allowed to be competitive with their pricing; therefore, each practice will charge different prices. This is the main factor for many owners when choosing a veterinarian; however, it should be the least important. Some veterinarians will allow for flexible payment options if an expensive emergency should arise, such as allowing a pet insurance company to pay them directly, or paying off the bill in installments.

Another financial aspect to look into is whether they offer a health plan. Some veterinarians set up monthly payments at discounted rates which will cover yearly check-ups, vaccinations, flea prevention, and worming treatments. This is often an excellent way of saving money over the course of the dog's life.

Off-Hours Services

Some veterinarians provide off-hours services on weekends and nighttime, while others delegate their services to their local off-hours veterinary provider. There are pros and cons of both, and it is up to you to decide which you prefer. Services provided by the practice themselves will allow continuity for the dog and owner, and potentially provide less stress in a scenario which is already stressful. However, a dedicated service often has veterinarians working for it which are specifically trained in emergency medicine, and therefore may be more skilled than the average general practitioner.

CHAPTER 11   Preventative Veterinary Medicine

Additional Services

Many veterinary practices also provide additional services, managed by veterinary nurses, such as puppy play parties, weight checks, flea checks, grooming services, holiday boarding, diabetic clinics, and dental clinics. For some owners, these are important factors when choosing a veterinarian.

Qualifications of the Veterinarian

The qualification status of the veterinarian may be a consideration for a new dog owner. Most veterinary practices will have the credentials of their veterinarians displayed on the walls and written on the website. A practice with certificate holders in advanced medicine, surgery, ophthalmology, or orthopedics may allow for more complicated procedures to be carried out onsite, rather than needing referral to a specialist veterinary practice.

Vaccinations

All puppies should have routine vaccinations every year. In their first year of life, this will involve several visits to the vets, and thereafter, just one visit per year.

The main diseases vaccinated against are as follows:

- Distemper – This vaccination is in the form of an injection. Distemper is a disease which causes coughing, sneezing, vomiting, diarrhea, lethargy, and reddened eyes, before it spreads to the brain and causes symptoms such as seizures. It also causes hardening of the pads and the nose.

- Hepatitis – This vaccination is in the form of an injection. Hepatitis is an inflammation of the liver caused by Canine Adenovirus. This causes symptoms such as abdominal pain, lethargy, diarrhea, vomiting, enlarged lymph nodes, loss of appetite, swelling of the brain, and eventually death.

- Parvovirus – This vaccination is in the form of an injection. Parvovirus is a life-threatening disease that is common among puppies. It causes profuse bloody diarrhea and occasionally vomiting. Puppies die rapidly of dehydration. It is extremely contagious.

- Leptospirosis – This vaccination is in the form of an injection. Up to four strains are vaccinated against depending on the vaccine brand. Dogs come into contact with Leptospirosis through contaminated water. It affects the kidneys, liver, central nervous system, and re-

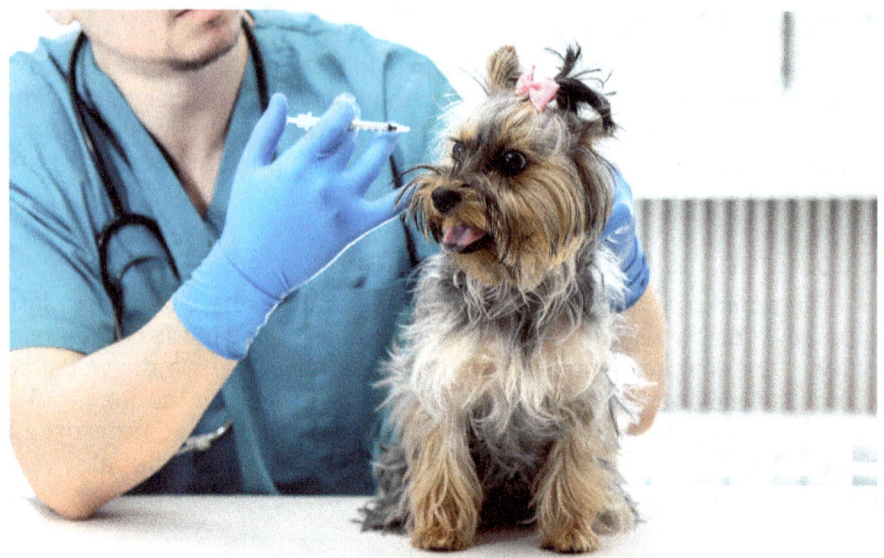

productive system and causes symptoms such as vomiting, diarrhea, lethargy, fever, and yellowing of the skin and eyes.
- Parainfluenza and Bordetella – These vaccinations are given in combination in a vaccine which squirts up a nostril of the dog. Together they form a complex disease called kennel cough. This is a highly contagious respiratory disease which causes an inflamed trachea, a hacking cough, and copious phlegm.
- Rabies – This vaccination is in the form of an injection. In rabies endemic areas, it is vital that this vaccination is given. Rabies is a very dangerous virus which can be transmitted to humans through bites. It causes excessive drooling, aggression, and behavior changes which rapidly progress to death within a week for 100% of cases showing clinical symptoms.

The vaccination schedule for these diseases may differ slightly depending on the manufacturer of the vaccination and the individual vet practice. Parvovirus, distemper, and hepatitis are usually all combined into one vaccine rather than given in individual injections.

There are a number of dog owners who believe vaccinations are not beneficial to the dog, and in fact, harmful to the dog. However, the chance of an adverse reaction is very low and the adjuncts which the vaccination is mixed with are not harmful to any animal. Vaccination companies advise on a schedule for repeat vaccinations, which is usually once every one, two, or three years, depending on the disease, but they are regularly an underestimation of how long it works to ensure the efficacy has not waxed and waned before the next injection. Therefore, to avoid over-vaccination, which poses no harm to the dog, there is the option of performing yearly blood tests to investigate the level of immunity still residing before topping up with another vaccination.

Microchipping

It is highly recommended that all dogs are microchipped at one of the initial vaccination appointments. In the event of your dog escaping, it will ease the process of reuniting him with you as the contact details can be acquired though a quick scan of the microchip.

The microchip is inserted via a needle in between the shoulder blades. The veterinarian will wipe the area clean before inserting it, then inject, which takes a matter of seconds.

Since Yorkshire Terriers are small, the needle in comparison to them is fairly large. Therefore, many will yelp on insertion of the needle, but the pain is very short-lived.

Neutering

All owners of dogs who are not going to be used for breeding or showing purposes should consider neutering their dogs. There are pros and cons to the neutering process; however, most will agree the pros will vastly outweigh the cons.

When a female dog is neutered, this is known as a spay or ovariohysterectomy, and when a male is neutered, this is known as a castration. Both are surgical procedures which require the dog to be at the vet practice for the day. Even though the Yorkshire Terrier is a small breed of dog, this does not make the surgical procedure any more difficult for the veterinarian.

Spaying

Spaying is recommended either before the first season, which is often experienced between nine and 15 months, or more than three months after the first season. Within the three months immediately after a season, the female dog will have a high concentration of hormones within the body and therefore the uterus will be swollen and more vas-

> **HELPFUL TIP**
> **An Ounce of Prevention**
>
> Unless you plan on breeding your Yorkie, spaying or neutering is advised. Female Yorkies benefit from spaying at an early age. Spaying reduces the risk of ovarian cancer and assists with the avoidance of "marking" tendencies. Neutering a male Yorkie eliminates the risk of testicular tumors and cancer. Up to 60 percent of unneutered male dogs over five years of age are symptomatic for enlarged prostates. Neutering also decreases the chances your Yorkie will run out in search of females. If breeding is in your sights, consult your vet to check if your Yorkie female is a good candidate for breeding.

cularized. This makes the surgery more difficult and puts the dog at risk of bleeding during the operation.

Spaying a female dog will eliminate seasons, and therefore also the mess that accompanies them around the house. It will also prevent unwanted pregnancies and attention from male dogs in the vicinity. However, the greatest health benefit for spaying is to prevent uterine infections, known as pyometras. A pyometra can be life threatening and is very common in entire female dogs.

Another health benefit is if the female dog is spayed early on in her life, the chances of mammary gland cancers are greatly reduced. Cancer of the mammary gland is hormonally driven, particularly by progesterone and estrogen, so by removing the ovaries, these hormones are not produced. In female dogs spayed before their first season, they will never have produced these hormones, and therefore the risk of mammary gland cancer is negligible; however, with every season, the risks of mammary cancer later in life increases.

The reason that some owners choose to spay their female dog after their first season, and allow some of these hormones to be exposed to the dog, is because estrogen tightens the urethral sphincter tone. The urethral sphincter is the band of muscle that opens and closes when the dog urinates or stops urinating. If it is lacking in tone, over the years it becomes leaky. Therefore, older female dogs who were spayed before their first season often exhibit mild urine leakage.

The spay operation may be performed a number of different ways depending on the veterinarian and their level of expertise and preference. Keyhole surgery is a possibility for this operation. This shortens recovery time as there is very little trauma; however, the time under anesthetic for the operation will be longer since the operation is more complicated. The operation can also be performed in the classical way, where an incision from the navel of the female dog will extend several centimeters toward the pelvis. During this operation the vet might take out both the ovaries and the uterus, or just the ovaries. The method used does not affect the benefits of spaying and the outcome will be the same.

Some minor negatives of spaying include the coat changing to a slightly coarser texture, and a decrease in metabolism. Due to the metabolism decrease, it is advised that spayed female dogs are fed less than non-spayed female dogs.

Castration

Castration holds many benefits for the male dog. It eliminates the risks of unwanted mating, and will improve the behavior of an aggressive or unruly dog. In addition, it will eliminate the chances of testicular and prostate cancers, and reduce the chances of prostate enlargement, known as benign prostate hyperplasia. This can lead to difficulty urinating and defecating.

The castration operation is usually performed after both testicles have descended into the scrotum. This is often between two and six months of age. Many owners opt to wait until the dog is in their second half year of life as then they are a little bigger and at less risk of developing a low blood glucose during the operation. Also, since Yorkshire Terriers are small in size, waiting a few more months will make the job of the surgeon easier.

Like spaying, castration will change the metabolism of the dog and therefore it is recommended that the calorie intake is carefully controlled to avoid obesity.

Internal Parasites

As discussed in Chapter 10, external parasite control is vital for the health of the animal. But internal parasite control is equally important.

Dogs can be prone to contracting several different types of internal parasites, namely tapeworms and roundworms. There are other internal parasites of the protozoa family, but these are more commonly found in puppies.

Both roundworms and tapeworms must be controlled on a regular basis through de-worming treatments. These can be in the form of pipettes on the back of the neck, which are often combined with external parasite medications, or in a form which can be ingested, such as a paste, tablet, or treat. It is recommended that roundworm treatment is given every month, as this will ensure cover for lungworm, which can be found inside slugs and snails. Other roundworms can be contracted through scavenging and contact with feces of other animals.

Tapeworms, like many roundworms, are also picked up through scavenging and contact with feces; however, unlike roundworms, the dog only needs to have a tapeworm treatment once every three to six months, depending on how often they scavenge.

Pet Insurance

Many new owners wonder if pet insurance is worth the money. Vet bills can be costly, and some major operations can cost thousands of dollars. It is rare that the average owner will have that money in savings. Pet insurance can be used for all vet bills and medications, apart from routine visits such as vaccinations.

Pet insurance can be provided in several different options, so it is important that if you are considering opening a policy, read the fine print. It could be offered as a pot of money which can be used every year for any condition, and is renewed at the end of each year, or it could be presented as an amount of money per condition to last for the lifetime of

CHAPTER 11 Preventative Veterinary Medicine

the animal, or finally it may be a sum of money per condition which is renewed every year. Policies will also differ in the amount of excess that is required to be paid depending on the policy chosen, the company, and the age of the dog.

Veterinary bills can easily cost thousands of dollars for unexpected surgeries, such as a fractured leg or ingestion of something that causes a blockage; therefore, if pet insurance is not taken out, it is wise to save for any unforeseen circumstances.

CHAPTER 12
Yorkshire Terrier Diseases

As Yorkshire Terriers go, they are generally a hardy little breed of dog. Like with all breeds of dog though, there are some diseases which Yorkies are more prone to than others. When owning a Yorkshire Terrier, it is a good idea to familiarize yourself with these diseases and be on the lookout for signs so that they can be addressed quickly.

Not all Yorkshire Terriers will go on to have these issues throughout their lifetime, so just because there is a higher prevalence within the breed, you should not worry yourself unnecessarily about them.

Dry Eye

Also known as keratoconjunctivitis sicca (KCS), dry eye is a disease which some Yorkshire Terriers may go on to develop. It can easily be overlooked because Yorkies often have discharge from their eyes, due to their long hair touching the eyes. This can be completely normal.

The medical term essentially means "inflammation of the cornea and surrounding tissues due to drying out." It is due to inadequate production of tears from the lacrimal gland and/or the tear gland in the third eyelid. This is usually due to immune-mediated destruction of the glands, or in other words, the body's own immune system attacking and destroying the glands.

Tears are needed to lubricate the eye and remove debris which may have come into contact with the eye surface. Tears are made up of water, mucus, and fatty substances. When there are not enough tears in the eye, the dog will have painful eyes and they may be red and squint or blink excessively. There is usually a discharge from the eye, which is the mucus part of the tears that no longer has water in it. This is what is usually confused with normal discharge caused by the hair occasionally touching the eye.

In severe cases, ulceration may also happen, which might lead to scarring of the eye or increased pigmentation. If it is very extensive, the eye may also have a blue hue to the outside of it. The eye will also have numerous tiny blood vessels going to the area where it is ulcerated to try to bring nutrients to the area to heal it. Both eyes are usually affected; however, one is often worse than the other.

Dry eye can be easily diagnosed based on the history, clinical signs, and a test called the Schirmer tear test. Any veterinarian can carry out this test in a matter of minutes at very little cost. It is a simple test, where a strip of blotting paper is placed under the bottom eyelid for one minute, and it measures the amount of tears produced and absorbed within that time frame.

There are two aims of treatment for dry eye; firstly, to increase tear production and secondly to replace the tears. There are several eye drops available which stop the body from attacking the tear glands, thereby allowing them to function again to some degree. These are usually used in combination with replacement tears to keep the eye moist. These drops require lifelong administration, although once any ulcers have healed up and the eye is less painful, the drops can usually be reduced to just several times per day, rather than every few hours.

> **HELPFUL TIP**
> **Know the Health Facts**
>
> Yorkshire Terriers are susceptible to knee joint issues, skin allergies, and dry eyes. Know the signs and talk to your veterinarian about these Yorkie-specific problem areas. One common problem that may occur in Yorkies is a collapsed trachea. The use of a harness rather than a collar is advised to avoid stress on the trachea and surrounding areas. Training your dog to walk next to you is a very important step to avoiding a collapsed trachea. Yorkies are speedy walkers and can pull ahead of their owners. Be proactive when it comes to the health and overall safety of your pet.

Patella Luxation

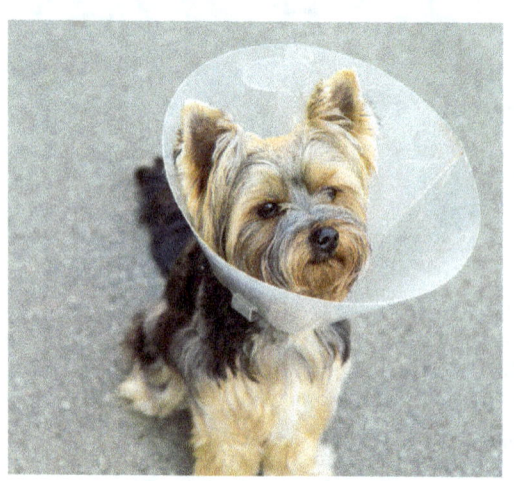

Yorkshire Terriers have the second highest prevalence of patella luxation out of all breeds, with about 26% of Yorkies having it in some form. It is an abnormality where the bones of the stifle have developed incorrectly, and therefore the patella (kneecap) can slip out of the groove in which it should be positioned. This can vary between individuals, and graded on a one to four basis. Grade one is where it slightly slips out and easily slips back in, and causes no pain at all to the dog. Grade four is where it slips out entirely and cannot be replaced back in the groove, which is painful and significantly reduces function of the joint. Most Yorkies which suffer from it will be somewhere in the middle.

The patella can slip out medially (to the inside) or laterally (to the outside), but medial displacement is the more common one. The most common symptoms are a non-painful intermittent skip when running; however, with increased severity, it can lead to chronic and persistent lameness. With time, since the joint is abnormal, it is likely to lead to arthritis, which is discussed in chapter 15.

Diagnosis is made through physical manipulation by the veterinarian, who is trained to be able to feel where the patella is. Some veterinarians will also take an X-ray to confirm what the joint looks like.

There are some options for surgical corrections if the luxation grade is high and the dog is still young. There are three main options with surgery; to tighten the ligaments surrounding the patella, to place a prosthetic ridge to make it harder for the patella to slip out, or to deepen the groove in which the patella sits, thereby keeping the patella more firmly in the groove. Some advanced cases in older dogs who have already developed arthritis will not be suitable for surgery and therefore the only option is to manage the associated pain if and when it occurs.

CHAPTER 12 Yorkshire Terrier Diseases

Collapsed Trachea

Of all the cases of collapsed tracheas, Yorkshire Terriers are over-represented, with approximately 65% of collapsed trachea cases being Yorkies.

The trachea is the windpipe that allows a smooth flow of air from the mouth, down to the lungs. It is held open via rings of cartilage at roughly half-centimeter spacings from the top to the bottom. Tracheal collapse is a progressive condition affecting the rings of the cartilage. The condition is suspected to be inherited, where the cartilage is softer and weaker than it should be. As a result, the rings can collapse and cause a temporary blockage or partial blockage of the windpipe.

Typical symptoms which may be seen include a harsh or dry cough, sometimes described as honking, and the dog may have noisy or labored breathing. It may be particularly evident in overweight dogs, or dogs which have underlying heart or lung problems. It also may be exacerbated when the dog is distressed, excited, or exercising.

Unfortunately, there is no cure for the disease. It is advised that dogs with tracheal collapse avoid exercise in hot weather, and if they are overweight, weight loss will make a significant difference. Avoiding the use of collars or high-necked harnesses will significantly improve the symptoms, as these put pressure on the front of the neck.

Medication can be given to suppress coughing and if there is inflammation or lots of mucus, medication can help with this too. There are surgical options, but the surgery can be tricky and is generally only performed when the dog cannot cope with medical management. This is usually done by inserting implants or stents, which mimic cartilage rings and are placed to keep the windpipe open.

Skin Allergies

Many breeds suffer from a tendency to develop skin allergies, and Yorkshire Terriers are certainly one of them. Allergies can be from three different sources: allergic to parasite bites, e.g., fleas; allergic to food; and allergic to environmental allergens. Often if a dog is allergic to one thing, they are allergic to many. It is a process of elimination to figure out which your dog is allergic to.

Allergies start to become apparent between the ages of one and three years old, and itchy skin is the main symptom. Dogs may chew, lick, or scratch their skin as an indication that they are itchy. It is usually itchy in specific and symmetrical areas, those areas being the paws, under the armpits, in the groin area, on the belly, and on the flanks. The skin in those areas may look completely normal, reddened, spotty (however without heads to the spot, as this is an indication of a skin infection), or with increased pigmentation. Other symptoms of an allergy may include recurrent ear infections and diarrhea.

Allergies can be diagnosed through several different means. The main method is a process of elimination. Firstly, all external parasites are ruled out. The veterinarian will check for parasites, and prescribe a parasite prevention treatment to be applied every four weeks. Next, food allergies are ruled out with a food trial. Hypoallergenic or anti-allergenic food is available through veterinary practices, where the proteins in it have been hydrolyzed. This means the body does not recognize the proteins and therefore does not respond to them. A food trial will last up to six weeks, and in this time, nothing but the food can be given.

If the dog still hasn't improved, then it can be assumed that the allergy is due to something in the environment. Blood tests can be carried out to understand exactly what the dog is allergic to, and if lucky, the allergy might be things which can be avoided, such as chicken feathers; however, often it is a number of things like grasses and pollens, which cannot be avoided. In that case there are several different options for management of the allergy.

The first option is for a course of steroid tablets or injections to bring down the inflammation. This is extremely cheap, at only a few cents per tablet, but there are huge side effects to steroids. The dog will feel very thirsty and hungry, and there is also a considerable toll on the liver and kidneys. Therefore, it is not recommended to keep a dog on steroids long term, but rather just use them in the case of a flare-up.

Steroids can also be provided in a local form, such as in creams or sprays, which are a good alternative to them being given internally, as only a limited amount of the steroid is absorbed.

Another option are tablets that suppress the immune system. These tablets have much fewer side effects, and are much kinder on the internal organs. However, the downside to these tablets is that they are quite expensive, at more than ten times the cost of steroids.

Finally, a therapy called immunomodulation is becoming more popular. This is where a laboratory creates a specific vaccination for a dog against exactly what they are allergic to. This vaccination is then administered by your vet at increasing intervals, firstly every couple of days, increasing to weeks, and finally being managed on roughly once every month. About 50% of dogs respond excellently to immunomodulation,

CHAPTER 12 Yorkshire Terrier Diseases

and the other 50% only have a partial improvement to their allergy, but it is the therapy with the fewest side effects.

There are no right or wrong treatment options for allergies, and different dogs will respond differently to each one, so it is often a process of trial and elimination.

For all of the conditions mentioned in this chapter, it is important to remember they are lifelong and will require chronic medication. It is useful if you have an excellent relationship with your vet, so find someone both you and your dog really like, so that you can work together to ensure the best outcome for everyone. These conditions are not the end of the world, and many owners with dogs with these conditions enjoy a happy, relatively healthy dog for the duration of their lifetime.

CHAPTER 13
Breeding

Breeding Yorkshire Terriers requires a wealth of knowledge and should not be taken lightly. Ideally it should only be carried out by professional breeding establishments. There are so many puppies in the world, so breeding just for fun because it would be nice to have a litter of puppies is not a responsible reason to breed your dog. However, if you are considering becoming a professional Yorkshire Terrier breeder, or you find your Yorkie has accidentally become pregnant and you wish to keep the pregnancy, then this chapter will provide a basic overview of what to expect.

Deciding about Breeding

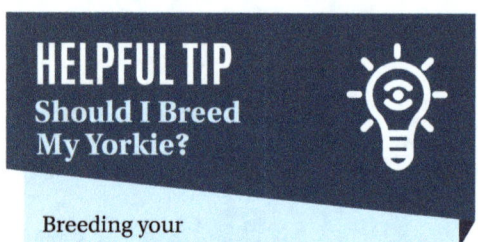

HELPFUL TIP
Should I Breed My Yorkie?

Breeding your Yorkshire Terrier can be a complicated endeavor. Don't be tempted to experiment on your own while breeding your dog. If done correctly, breeding dogs can be a rewarding experience. It should, however, be left to the experts. If your Yorkie is a loving pet and home companion, the benefits of spaying and neutering should not be overlooked. Do your homework, research, and ask experts for advice before attempting to breed your dog.

Yorkie breeding, if done well, can be very rewarding. Improving the bloodlines and making a name for yourself in the breeding world is an exciting prospect, and this is the main objective for many breeders. It is important to also aim toward breeding healthy puppies that conform to the American Kennel Club standards, and raising them to be happy and socialized, while also maintaining the health of the parents.

If you are considering breeding Yorkies as a business, you should be aware that to create an ethical and caring establishment, a lot of money must first be invested. Breeders will make a bit of profit from the puppies, but many people will run a breeding establishment as a second income and not for their sole income. Breeding will not make you rich.

CHAPTER 13   Breeding

Mating

It is recommended that females are only bred after their second heat and should not be older than five years old at the time of mating. If she has started her seasons young, and not yet fully grown by her second heat, waiting until she has reached that size will make sure she will be able to cope with the stresses that pregnancy can bring. After five years old, the body takes more strain from the pregnancy, and complications can arise, such as the need for caesarean sections and infections. She should be retired and spayed after her third litter.

Yorkshire Terriers are small dogs, so when choosing a suitable mating partner, the size of the dogs should be considered. A small female mated to a large male may have complications during birth if the puppies have inherited their father's large body size. This is why the female should always weigh more than the male.

The Yorkshire Terrier's cycle lasts approximately 21 days and occurs every six months. Outside of these 21 days, hormones are maintained at a baseline and everything is inactive. All dogs are different though, and so keeping a calendar to determine your dog's cycle will make the mating process easier to predict.

The female can be mated when she shows signs of being in heat, which may only be for a few days in the 21-day cycle. Signs include a leak of clear fluid for a few days, followed by a change to blood or light pink fluid for several more days. The vulva may also become moderately enlarged. Some females will also exhibit a nesting behavior, and be clingier over their owner or over a specific toy. After the symptoms stop, she may still be in heat for a few more days, and this can be evident by touching the base of her tail; if she moves it to one side, she is still in heat.

She should visit the stud dog during the time she is in heat, and under supervision they can be mated. During the mating process, the male dog turns around so that they are facing away from each other. This is called a tie, and once they are tied, they cannot be separated without considerable damage to the male.

Pregnancy

Once mated, a Yorkshire Terrier will be pregnant for an average of 63 days. A pregnancy can be confirmed with a blood test after day 22 or by day 42 via an ultrasound scan. It is impossible to be certain how many puppies are in the mother unless an X-ray is carried out after day

45, which is when the puppies' bones have calcified; however, this can be harmful to the development of the puppies and so is not routinely done.

Signs of pregnancy include the mother acting sleepy, grooming herself more than usual, and gathering items to make a nest. Her abdomen may feel firmer than usual, and toward the end start to bulge, and the nipples will rapidly grow. After four weeks, her appetite will increase and it is important to feed her more, as she will be using a lot of energy to provide the puppies with all the nutrients they need. She will also gain roughly 30% of her ideal weight during pregnancy.

During pregnancy, everyone who comes into contact with the mother should be very gentle with her. She should have a warm and comfy area to rest, where it is quiet and she will not be disturbed. She should still be encouraged to exercise, but a 15-to-20-minute walk with limited jumping and running is all that is needed.

Birthing

Taking your Yorkie's temperature twice a day toward the end of the pregnancy will enable you to understand what her normal temperature is. When it suddenly drops, labor is likely to start within 24 hours. The temperature should be taken with a canine rectal thermometer, gently inserted with plenty of lubrication. A dog's normal temperature should be between 101 and 102.5 degrees Fahrenheit, and may drop below 100 degrees Fahrenheit before she gives birth.

When she starts labor, she may stop eating and may even vomit. This is normal and not a sign of illness. Contractions may cause her to whine, and a close eye should be kept on her to make sure it is all going smoothly. Most births will require very little or even no intervention from the owner.

Nevertheless, it is important to know when things are going wrong, and be quick to act if there are complications. These can include being pregnant for more than 70 days, it has been 24 hours since the temperature dropped and there have not been any puppies, one puppy has come out and it has been over two hours and no more have made an appearance (if you know there is more than one puppy), the mother is in extreme pain, there is excessive blood, or she is showing signs of weakness or extreme distress. In any of these cases, she must immediately be rushed to an emergency veterinarian. It may be the case that a caesarean section will be needed to remove the puppies surgically.

For delivery, the mother should be placed in a whelping box when the first signs of labor begin. This can be a large cardboard box with only three sides, or a dog bed without the cushion, and lined with towels or lots of layers of clean newspaper. Layers are a good idea as you can pull them out if they become soiled to keep the whelping box as clean as possible.

Sometimes puppies will come out quickly, one after another, but it can be normal for there to be intervals of up to two hours. Longer than this can indicate a puppy has become stuck or the mother has become exhausted. Each puppy will be born encased in the amniotic sac. Sometimes this will rip open when the puppy is passed through the birth canal, but more often it will be gently torn open by the mother when she has pushed out the puppy entirely. Once a puppy comes out, the mother will usually be able to cope with cleaning the puppy herself; however, many breeders prefer to help the mother by picking up the puppy and rubbing them vigorously on their back with a towel to stimulate breathing. This also dries and warms them. The mouth should also be emptied of any amniotic fluid. They then place the puppy by the head end of the mother so she can continue to clean and bond.

After all the puppies have been passed, the mother will usually eat the umbilical cords, amniotic sac, placenta, and any other birthing material. While this might seem a little unappetizing, it is full of nutrients to give the mother a boost after the tiring birthing process.

The puppies should start to nurse soon after all of them have been passed. You should monitor the puppies during this process to make sure all can suckle successfully, and none are getting bullied and pushed aside by the others. In some cases, the runt of the litter may need to be bottle fed.

The mother and puppies should then be allowed to rest and feed on clean bedding and a warm, not hot, heating pad placed under the blanket.

Aftercare

Once all settled, the mother can be given a warm sponge bath to keep her clean, and offered food and water. She may not be immediately hungry afterward, but food and water should be freely available to her at all times.

She will have some light discharge for about a week after birth, which might be pink, red, or brown. If it is green or black, excessive, or smelly,

Photo Courtesy of Nadia du Toit

then a vet should be contacted immediately, as this could be an indication of an infection or a dead puppy still left in the mother.

The temperature of the whelping box should be regulated at 85 degrees Fahrenheit during week one, and 82 degrees Fahrenheit during weeks two and three to make sure the puppies do not chill. There should also be no drafts nearby.

If the puppies are going to have their tails docked for show purposes, this should be done in the first three days of life by someone experienced in docking tails. Docking tails for showing in the USA is a requirement; however, it results in disqualification from some international shows, such as in the UK, so be sure this is what you want to do before making this irreversible change.

Several days after the birth, all puppies and mother should be examined by a veterinarian to ensure that the mother is healthy, and that no puppies have a cleft palate, umbilical hernia, or heart murmur.

CHAPTER 13   Breeding

Raising Puppies

Prospective new owners can come to view the puppies from a few weeks old, assuming all puppies are healthy and the mother is happy. New owners should be vetted to make sure they can provide a suitable home for a puppy. They may decide to reserve a puppy and put a deposit down to make sure nobody else chooses that puppy. When that happens, it is a good idea to put a collar on that puppy so that it can be distinguished from the rest, if it doesn't have distinctive markings.

If both parents are registered with the Kennel Club in your country, the litter may be registered online straight after the birth. Prompt registration is advisable so that the new owners can receive Kennel Club papers with their puppy when they collect it. They can then transfer ownership into their own names.

Puppies will need to remain with their mother up until at least eight weeks, and many breeders will not release a puppy before 12 weeks. When they are four weeks old, they may start showing interest in their mother's food, as well as drinking milk. This is when a commercial wet puppy food or soaked dry puppy food can be offered. At between six and eight weeks, they will cease to suckle, and eat the puppy food as their main source of nutrition.

At eight weeks old, the puppies can receive their first vaccinations. Sometimes they will also be microchipped at this stage; however, if they haven't yet been reserved by prospective new owners, the details will need to be registered to the breeder and will require being changed when the puppy is bought. Puppies also should be wormed against roundworms at 2, 4, 6, 8, and 12 weeks of age. They do not need to be treated against fleas during this time, but if any are spotted, a flea spray which is appropriate for their age should be used. Many flea treatments cannot be used on puppies under eight weeks old.

It can be rewarding to breed your own Yorkshire Terrier and produce a litter of puppies which are of good genetics and close to the breed standard, but it should be not taken with a light heart. The welfare of the mother is utmost, and for the inexperienced it is advisable to leave breeding up to the professional breeders.

CHAPTER 14
Showing

The Yorkshire Terrier is a very distinctive breed and can be presented in many ways according to the owner's preference, from scruffy to fashionable to highly polished. Naturally you would assume that to show your Yorkie you would have to follow the breed standard, which is very prescriptive, but if the idea of showing your cute scruffball for fun appeals to you, there are always small local shows with novelty classes, such as "Dog the Judge Would Most Like to Take Home." And how could any judge resist a Yorkie? So, entering fun shows can be a good, low-pressure way to show off your dog's individual appeal and meet other owners—and their dogs, of course!

If showing appeals to you, and you anticipate taking it further, entering the breed classes at local dog shows is a good introduction. These are broad groups such as "Terriers" rather than Yorkshire Terriers specifically. You will get your dog used to the show ring, being handled, and being on his best behavior around people and other dogs, as well as learning what will be required as you move up in the showing world. Making contacts and taking the advice of experienced show people will provide a useful support network for the future as your dog progresses.

CHAPTER 14   Showing

Selecting a Dog for Showing

If you intend to show your dog at a high level, you will most likely be choosing a puppy, and in this case the pedigrees of the parents will be important. Your Yorkshire Terrier will have to be registered with the American or British Kennel Club, or its equivalent in your country, and cannot come from undocumented breeding.

You should familiarize yourself with the breed standard before selecting your dog, as certain colorations or markings will disqualify the dog from Kennel Club shows, so he will only ever be a companion animal with the prospect of winning ribbons at local fun shows. Certain future characteristics of appearance will require a bit of vision at the puppy stage, and if you are not experienced with the breed, it will be well worth taking someone along with you who is. If you do not have such a contact, the breeder themselves should be able to advise which of the litter has show potential.

Coloration is the most obvious feature to determine your choice of puppy for the show ring, but as Yorkshire Terrier puppies are born black and tan, and the show standard is blue and tan, you will need to see the parents to evaluate how the puppy's coloration will develop. Dogs with white patches should only be selected as companion animals as they will not meet the show breed standard.

Character is an important requirement in a show dog. The Yorkshire Terrier should be confident and self-important. Therefore, look for a puppy that is showing these characteristics. If the parents have been successful show dogs, they should have passed on winning character traits to their offspring.

After Selecting Your Puppy

It is important to be aware that the purpose of showing has traditionally been to identify the optimum breeding stock for the perpetuation of quality and improvement in the breed. Therefore, show dogs are traditionally required to be unneutered.

The American Kennel Club is very clear that neutered dogs are disqualified from participating in conformation classes. They may, however, take part in performance events.

The British Kennel Club does grant exceptions, but requires a "Permission to Show" letter, available by application on its website. With a male, the standard requirement of two testicles, fully descended into the scrotum, may therefore be certified as having been present before being removed, so the dog was effectively perfect. In practice, many feel that their neutered dog, although allowed to compete in the UK with a "Permission to Show" letter, would be placed higher if unneutered.

Normally, spaying a female dog is always recommended if the bitch is not intended to breed, to avoid the risk of pyometra and unwanted pregnancies. However, show females are rarely spayed, as apart from maintaining their value as breeding animals, the coat is known to change and become coarser after the procedure. These two factors are likely to prejudice the dog's chances in higher-level dog shows. In the USA, a spayed female would be disqualified from AKC conformation shows.

Tail docking is a procedure historically intended to avoid damage to the tail in a working dog that might get caught on undergrowth. It subsequently became fashionable even in companion and show dogs when there was no practical need for the tail to be short.

In the UK, tail docking is now illegal, except for certain working breeds, of which the Yorkshire Terrier is not one. Therefore, if a Yorkie born after 2007 is docked, he will not be allowed to enter high-level shows in the United Kingdom, even if he is a champion in another coun-

CHAPTER 14 Showing

try. This rule only applies to shows where the public are admitted on payment of a fee, such as Crufts.

In the USA, however, tail docking is still a breed requirement of the American Kennel Club, and the tail should be docked to medium length.

The disparity in requirements relating to docking and neutering between the UK and USA therefore will determine the decisions made for your Yorkshire Terrier puppy, as you will need to comply with the rules pertaining to the country in which you wish to show your dog.

Apart from the more irreversible decisions you may have to make with your puppy if he or she is to be a show dog, you will have to accustom him at an early age to being handled and groomed, as his coat will need to be maintained by brushing and pulling rather than clipping and cutting, to preserve its silky texture. Obedience classes will condition your dog to being around other dogs and people, and teach him the basics that he will need in the ring. There are also ringcraft classes that will teach handling for prospective show dogs. You may like to get out to a few shows as a spectator while your puppy is still too young to compete, to get a feel for what is required. Your Yorkshire Terrier can then begin his career at six months, with conformation classes for puppies where you can both learn the basics as a springboard for the future.

Registering your puppy with the Kennel Club in his country is not only a requirement for serious pedigree showing, but will give you access to information about shows through which your dog can win points toward qualifying for large championship shows such as Crufts.

Remember, your dog is not competing against other dogs for being the prettiest; the strict criterion for a winning dog is that he or she conforms to the breed standard. It is actually detrimental to the breed if the dog has stand-out characteristics. This is all ultimately for the reason that showing is about the ability of the dog to produce puppies that will also meet the breed standard. Consequently, this blueprint needs to be the most important reference point for anyone showing their dog in conformation classes. If your dog does not meet this standard, he can still be a champion in performance and fun classes.

Breed Standard

The breed standard for the Yorkshire Terrier differs between countries so it is important to look up the current requirement in the country in which you wish to show. With the USA and the UK being the largest showing centers, the show standards are given here:

The American Kennel Club Official Standard of the Yorkshire Terrier (2007)

General Appearance:

That of a long-haired toy terrier whose blue and tan coat is parted on the face and from the base of the skull to the end of the tail and hangs evenly and quite straight down each side of body. The body is neat, compact and well proportioned. The dog's high head carriage and confident manner should give the appearance of vigor and self-importance.

Head:

Small and rather flat on top, the skull not too prominent or round, the muzzle not too long, with the bite neither undershot nor overshot and teeth sound. Either scissors bite or level bite is acceptable. The nose is black. Eyes are medium in size and not too prominent; dark in color and sparkling with a sharp, intelligent expression. Eye rims are dark. Ears are small, V-shaped, carried erect and set not too far apart.

Body:

Well-proportioned and very compact. The back is rather short, the backline level, with height at shoulder the same as at the rump.

Legs and Feet:

Forelegs should be straight, elbows neither in nor out. Hind legs straight when viewed from behind, but stifles are moderately bent when viewed from the sides. Feet are round with black toenails. Dewclaws, if any, are generally removed from the hind legs. Dewclaws on the forelegs may be removed.

Tail:

Docked to a medium length and carried slightly higher than the level of the back.

Coat:

Quality, texture and quantity of coat are of prime importance. Hair is glossy, fine and silky in texture. Coat on the body is moderately long and perfectly straight (not wavy). It may be trimmed to floor length to give ease of movement and a neater appearance, if desired. The fall on the head is long, tied with one bow in center of head or parted in the middle

CHAPTER 14   Showing

and tied with two bows. Hair on muzzle is very long. Hair should be trimmed short on tips of ears and may be trimmed on feet to give them a neat appearance.

Colors:

Puppies are born black and tan and are normally darker in body color, showing an intermingling of black hair in the tan until they are matured. Color of hair on body and richness of tan on head and legs are of prime importance in adult dogs, to which the following color requirements apply: Blue - Is a dark steel-blue, not a silver-blue and not mingled with fawn, bronzy or black hairs. Tan - All tan hair is darker at the roots than in the middle, shading to still lighter tan at the tips. There should be no sooty or black hair intermingled with any of the tan.

Color on Body:

The blue extends over the body from back of neck to root of tail. Hair on tail is a darker blue, especially at end of tail.

Headfall:

A rich golden tan, deeper in color at sides of head, at ear roots and on the muzzle, with ears a deep rich tan. Tan color should not extend down on back of neck.

Chest and Legs:

A bright, rich tan, not extending above the elbow on the forelegs nor above the stifle on the hind legs.

Weight:

Must not exceed seven pounds.

Disqualifications:

Any solid color or combination of colors other than blue and tan as described above. Any white markings other than a small white spot on the forechest that does not exceed 1 inch at its longest dimension.

The British Kennel Club Official Standard of the Yorkshire Terrier (2009)

General Appearance:
Long-coated, coat hanging quite straight and evenly down each side, a parting extending from nose to end of tail. Very compact and neat, carriage very upright conveying an important air. General outline conveying impression of vigorous and well-proportioned body.

Characteristics:
Alert, intelligent toy terrier.

Temperament:
Spirited with even disposition.

Head and Skull:
Rather small and flat, not too prominent or round in skull, nor too long in muzzle; black nose.

Eyes:
Medium, dark, sparkling, with sharp intelligent expression and placed to look directly forward. Not prominent. Edge of eyelids dark.

Ears:
Small, V-shaped, carried erect, not too far apart, covered with short hair, color very deep, rich tan.

Mouth:
Perfect, regular and complete scissor bite, i.e. upper teeth closely overlapping lower teeth and set square to the jaws. Teeth well placed with even jaws.

Neck:
Good reach.

Forequarters:
Well laid shoulders, legs straight, well covered with hair of rich golden tan a few shades lighter at ends than at roots, not extending higher on forelegs than elbow.

Body:
Compact with moderate spring of rib, good loin. Level back.

Hindquarters:
Legs quite straight when viewed from behind, moderate turn of stifle. Well

CHAPTER 14 Showing

covered with hair of rich golden tan a few shades lighter at ends than at roots, not extending higher on hindlegs than stifles.

Feet:
Round; nails black.

Tail:
Previously customarily docked.

Docked: Medium length with plenty of hair, darker blue in color than rest of body, especially at end of tail. Carried a little higher than level of back.

Undocked: Plenty of hair, darker blue in color than rest of body, especially at end of tail. Carried a little higher than level of back. As straight as possible.

Length to give a well-balanced appearance.

Gait/Movement:
Free with drive; straight action front and behind, retaining level topline.

Coat:
Hair on body moderately long, perfectly straight (not wavy), glossy; fine silky texture, not woolly, must never impede movement. Fall on head long, rich golden tan, deeper in color at sides of head, about ear roots and on muzzle where it should be very long. Tan on head not to extend on to neck, nor must any sooty or dark hair intermingle with any of tan.

Color:
Dark steel blue (not silver blue), extending from occiput to root of tail, never mingled with fawn, bronze or dark hairs. Hair on chest rich, bright tan. All tan hair darker at the roots than in middle, shading to still lighter at tips.

Size:
Weight up to 3.2 kgs (7 lbs.).

Faults:
Any departure from the foregoing points should be considered a fault and the seriousness with which the fault should be regarded should be in exact proportion to its degree and its effect upon the health and welfare of the dog and on the dog's ability to perform its traditional work.

Note:
Male animals should have two apparently normal testicles fully descended into the scrotum.

Preparing for a Show

FUN FACT
Ratter Turned Show Dog

Although originally bred to ferret out rats in English and Scottish mills and mines, the Yorkshire Terrier grew to be one of the most beloved dogs in the world. It is believed that Clydesdale, Paisley, and Skye terriers were the building breeds of the Yorkshire Terrier. The breed has developed into an exceptional show dog in the toy breed class because of its intelligence, curiosity, and its ability to work a crowd. This "little dog that could" always receives cheers of love and gratitude from adoring crowds at dog shows.

So, you have selected your puppy carefully, registered him with the Kennel Club in your country, socialized him, and trained him to be of a stable temperament, obedient in a busy environment, and comfortable with being handled. What next?

You may learn of upcoming dog shows through posters on the vet's notice board, newspaper ads, word of mouth, or the Kennel Club's website. Once you have your sights set on a show, you need to contact the show secretary for a copy of the schedule, and identify which class or classes you would like to enter. Complete the form and send it off with your payment, and you're good to go.

A few days before the show, you should bathe your dog to remove excess oils and condition his coat. Trim his nails so they do not touch the ground. Yorkies are prone to excessively long nails so regular trimming is important to keep the quick short. Groom your dog thoroughly so that you are not dealing with any matted fur or flakes of dry skin on the day.

Think about travel arrangements if the show is not local. If your dog gets car sick, you may need to travel in advance and book dog-friendly accommodations. Take a comfortable crate that the dog feels at home in, so he has somewhere familiar to relax. You will need leashes and a badge or armband to put a number card in, and the handler will need a plain-colored comfortable suit so the judge can see the outline of the dog clearly against your legs.

On the day, you will need to be especially attentive to the Yorkshire Terrier's crowning glory, his long coat. This should be floor length on a show dog. It is commonplace to use straighteners on the coat of a Yorkie, but always lodge a comb into the hair near the root to ensure you do not burn the skin.

CHAPTER 14   Showing

Photo Courtesy of
High 'N Yorkies
Photographer PERVENCEVA ELENA

Apply grooming sprays to the brush rather than the coat, to ensure even distribution. Likewise, when it comes to backcombing the top knot, apply hairspray to the comb and then to the hair. This is the finishing embellishment to your show dog, and there are plenty of online videos to help you create the perfect top knot, which should be finished with a red ribbon.

You may carry a brush in the ring to ensure your dog looks his best when awaiting the judge.

So now all that is left is to enjoy the show, and hopefully win a ribbon. But remember it is poor show etiquette to ever question the judge's decision. If your beautifully turned out dog does not win on this occasion, there is always next time!

CHAPTER 15
Living with a Senior Dog

Aging is a natural part of life. Most people own a dog for their dog's entire life, and as a result, at some point the dog will become senior. Different dogs are considered senior at different points in their lives; while a large dog may be considered senior at six or seven years old, Yorkshire Terriers have a longer life expectancy than many breeds, and may still act young and spritely well into their double figures. It is still worth treating your Yorkshire Terrier of over 10 years old as senior though.

Older dogs are more prone to health issues, and to extend their quality of life, you should become familiar with these problems. It is impossible to avoid some of these health problems; however, by careful management and regular check-ups with a veterinarian, the dog's quality of life can be extended significantly.

Photo Courtesy of Ryanne Seldon

Diet Change

All Yorkshire Terriers over the age of 10 should be placed on a senior dog diet. Most major commercial diets offer a senior option, and these diets are extremely beneficial to an older dog.

Senior diets are often based around the adult dog diets, with similar recipes, but some major differences. The first difference is usually the calorie content of the diet. Older dogs have a slower metabolism than younger dogs, and due to decreasing mobility with age, it is common to see an overweight older dog. This in turn puts stress on already compromised joints and organs, and creates a deteriorating cycle. Senior diets will have a lower calorie content, to stop unnecessary weight gain. Some will also have a higher fiber content to improve satiety, so that the dog doesn't feel hungry due to receiving fewer calories.

Senior diets often include increased concentrations of fatty acids, such as omega-3 and omega-6. These fatty acids have a scientifically proven effect on decreasing inflammation, and are commonly used as part of a treatment protocol for dogs with joint problems. Not only do they decrease joint inflammation, they are also vital for skin and brain health, both of which can deteriorate with age.

Senior diets may also be slightly easier to eat than adult diets, both in terms of palatability and texture. Older dogs may become fussier with age, and in combination with deteriorating dentition, sometimes it can be a struggle to encourage them to eat. Some senior diets attempt to tackle this through changing the taste or texture of the food.

Finally, many senior diets have added glucosamine. This is a compound which improves joint cartilage, primarily through increasing production of glycosaminoglycans (GAGs). GAGs improve the make-up of cartilage and the joint's ability to bear forces, resulting in less damage to cartilage cells which may be affected by arthritic changes. This will be further discussed later in this chapter.

> **HELPFUL TIP**
> **Be Your Dog's Best Advocate**
>
> As you watch your Yorkie age, you will notice changes in health, diet, and sleep patterns. Perhaps more frequent trips to the vet may be required as a dog ages. Reevaluate your dog's exercise needs as he gets older. Consult your veterinarian about dietary adaptations for your senior pet. A dog's best friend is his owner, and the time may come when you must make some heartbreaking decisions. Always be cognizant of quality of life for your companion.

Senior Wellness Checks

Photo Courtesy of Lacy Spinelli

As your dog reaches senior age, it is recommended to adhere to regular senior wellness checks at the vet. This could be either a yearly check-up or every 6 months, depending on how many underlying issues your dog might have.

At a senior wellness check, a vet will start with a physical exam of your Yorkie. This will include looking in the eyes, listening to the lungs and the heart, feeling the abdomen, checking the teeth, feeling all the joints, and checking for any lumps. After this, once a year, a blood test will usually be performed. This gives useful information about the health of internal organs which are affected by age, such as the liver or kidneys. Sometimes a blood pressure check will also be included, which requires a cuff around a leg to be inflated, and then when the pressure is released, a machine measures at which point the pulse returns.

Senior wellness checks may seem unnecessary to many owners who have healthy elderly dogs; however, by catching issues early in their course, early interventions can significantly slow down any deterioration and extend the lifespan of your Yorkie.

Many insurance companies will cover the cost of senior wellness checks, so it is worth contacting them to understand what exactly is covered on the policy. Veterinary insurance for elderly dogs is very useful, as most elderly dogs will end up being placed on some sort of chronic medication. You should thoroughly read the fine print, though, as usually the co-pay on the policy will increase with age, so a company that may have been excellent for younger dogs might not still be the best company for a senior dog. However, changing insurance companies when your Yorkie has reached a senior age is likely not in your best interests, as there may now be pre-existing conditions which you could be penalized for. Therefore, it is worth thinking in advance when taking out insurance, and look for a cover which will benefit you and your dog throughout their lifetime.

CHAPTER 15   Living with a Senior Dog

Arthritis

Almost all dogs in the latter half of their life will develop osteoarthritis, also known as just arthritis. Arthritis is usually characterized by visible limping, especially after rest, and a creaking or crunching feeling in the joints when flexed or extended. However, arthritic changes start long before these symptoms, so by the time lameness is evident, the dog is no longer in a mild stage, but rather in a moderate or severe stage of arthritis.

Arthritis usually happens in the shoulder, elbow, wrist, hip, stifle, or lumbosacral joints. It is due to either abnormal forces on a normal joint, for example if the dog is overweight, or normal forces on an abnormal joint, for example a Yorkshire Terrier which has had patella luxation all of its life.

Arthritis is a whole joint disease where many parts of the joint are affected. At the end of each long bone, the bone type becomes subchondral bone. This is a spongier part of the bone and it is that part which bears concussive forces when the leg hits the ground. On top of the subchondral bone is a layer of cartilage, which is smooth and helps the joints glide nicely. Finally, in between the two ends of the bones which are meeting in the joint, is joint fluid, known as synovial fluid, which is a viscous fluid. This aids as lubrication to the joint.

When a joint is arthritic, the cartilage and subchondral bone becomes destroyed, and the synovial fluid decreases in volume. This creates a grating joint, which is extremely painful. Unfortunately, arthritis cannot be reversed, but the progression can be successfully and significantly slowed.

Photo Courtesy of *Laura Ruckel*

There are five ways that arthritis can be tackled, and each way acts synergistically with another to enhance its effects, so, for example, 1+1 does not equal 2, but rather it equals 3, because they have enhanced each other. Many owners do not realize this, and just choose one method of controlling arthritis, which is not the most beneficial way of treating arthritis for your dog.

Pain Relief

There are several pain relief options on the market. The first line pain relief that is usually given is called a non-steroidal anti-inflammatory (NSAID). These are extremely effective, but should be given at the lowest effective dose, as they require the liver and kidneys to work harder than usual, and for some dogs they cause stomach upset.

If the dog has a compromised liver or kidney, or the guts do not tolerate NSAIDs, then other options for drugs are explored, such as opioids, gabapentin, or amantadine. These drugs can have an effect on the mental state of your dog, though, and can cause them to become a little spaced out.

Nutraceuticals

In conjunction with drugs, nutraceuticals are advised. These can be in the form of tablets, capsules, liquids, or pre-formulated diets with them added in. Nutraceuticals are natural supplements which have a major effect on the joints. They do not have any known side effects and are an excellent way of protecting the cartilage from deteriorating further. Common nutraceuticals include glucosamine, chondroitin, or green-lipped mussel, and all these have had hundreds of scientific studies which prove their effectiveness. Other popular but less researched nutraceuticals include MSM and turmeric, which also appear to be beneficial to arthritic joints.

Weight Loss

A scientific study looked at the difference between arthritis prevalence in lean-fed dogs versus a full-fat diet fed to dogs for their entire lifetime, and revealed that the lean-fed dogs had a prevalence of 50% arthritis by the end of their life, versus the full-fat-diet dogs having a prevalence of 83%. Therefore, by keeping the weight of your Yorkie down throughout its lifetime, the chances of him developing arthritis is significantly less.

However, arthritis progresses quickly in overweight dogs; therefore, even if your dog already has arthritis, losing weight is still beneficial. Due to decreased mobility, increasing the exercise might not be possible, but a low-calorie satiety diet will aid in weight loss without the feeling of hunger. Alternatively, asking a veterinarian to calculate the number of calories needed to be consumed based on the ideal weight, rather than the current weight, will allow for the same food to be given, but in a calculated quantity.

Omega Oils

As previously discussed, fatty acids such as omega-3 and omega-6 have proven anti-inflammatory properties. Whenever there is damage in the body, prostaglandins are produced by the body. These are known as inflammatory mediators, and cause the area to be inflamed, which leads to pain. Omega oils cause a prostaglandin called PGE3 to be produced, rather than PGE2, which is less inflammatory than PGE2 and therefore the inflammation is decreased.

Omega oils can be found in many foods, or can be given as pre-formulated supplements. Ingredients of dog food which are naturally high in omega oils are fish, flaxseed, hemp seeds, and coconut oil.

Physical Rehabilitation

Physical rehabilitation should always be carried out by a licensed professional; however, most professionals will also provide exercises to do with your dog at home too. Physical rehabilitation may take the form of physiotherapy, hydrotherapy, or acupuncture.

Physiotherapy is a therapy which builds up strength in supporting muscles, enabling the body to cope better with the strain from the diseased joint. This will be done through physical manipulation and massage, and the physiotherapist will almost certainly provide exercises to be carried out at home in between sessions as well.

Hydrotherapy is not simply swimming; it will also include exercises such as underwater treadmills to build up muscles. Hydrotherapy is an excellent form of exercise for dogs with arthritis, as the water takes some of the strain from the joints while providing resistance for the muscles.

Acupuncture is an ancient Chinese medicine which is now becoming more recognized in Western veterinary medicine as well. Extremely fine needles are placed in strategic points to release endorphins. These are natural pain relievers, and also relax any tight muscles.

Dementia

Many older dogs will start to develop canine cognitive dysfunction (CCD), which is similar to dementia in humans. There are areas of the brain which no longer work as effectively, and frequently the mental state of the dog changes.

The symptoms will differ from dog to dog, but may include tiredness, a change in personality, aimless wandering, urinating or defecating indoors when previously housebroken, or waking up in the middle of the night and thinking it is the morning.

Some owners choose to accept that this is part of aging; however, there are safe medications available which increase the blood flow to the brain and improve some of these symptoms.

Organ Deterioration

It is normal for dogs as they reach their senior years not to have optimal function of all of their organs any more. It does not necessarily mean that medication is necessary, but it must be kept in mind when considering some medications, diets, or exercise requirements.

The four most common organs to be affected are the kidneys, liver, lungs, and heart. The kidneys filter out toxins and waste products from the blood, as well as excess water, and this creates urine. When kidneys begin to deteriorate, blood can back up from them in the blood vessels, which in turn creates a high blood pressure. Other common symptoms include increased thirst and increased urination. Apart from the symptoms, a blood test can give a lot of detail about the health of the kidneys, and there are excellent medications to relieve the strain on them and improve their ability to function.

The liver is an organ with many functions; it produces bile which aids in digestion, it converts protein into a usable form, it excretes excess bilirubin into the guts, it plays a role in glucose storage, and it reduces toxins within the body. The first indication of a deteriorating liver is usually an incidental finding on a routine senior wellness blood test. Other symptoms which may be evident are a yellowing of the gums or eyes, due to an increase of bilirubin in the blood, or a swelling of the belly due to an increased size of the liver. There are excellent diets available for dogs with liver disease, which have small quantities of high-quality protein in, and supplements to aid in its day-to-day functioning as well.

The lungs of most dogs will change over time and there is very little that can be done to prevent this. Known as "old dog lungs," this can be seen on an X-ray as increased areas of white, which is scarring. The lungs lose their elasticity, and therefore are less springy than usual. In a healthy dog, this doesn't affect their quality of life much, but it does lead to an increased susceptibility to lung infections, and decreased ability to clear them effectively. Cancers are also common in older dogs, and the lungs are the first place cancer spreads to, so coughing in senior dogs should not be overlooked.

CHAPTER 15   Living with a Senior Dog

Finally, the heart can deteriorate in older dogs, and specifically in Yorkshire Terriers, the usual issue is a leaky mitral valve. The mitral valve is a valve in the left side of the heart which prevents back flow, so if it is leaking, then the heart has to pump much harder to push blood around the body. As a result, the heart enlarges, and a murmur can be heard through a veterinarian's stethoscope. Excellent drugs are available to reduce the burden on the heart, increase its ability to pump, and maintain a normal blood pressure.

Loss of Senses

A common problem that owners of elderly dogs encounter is loss of the senses; mainly loss of hearing or loss of sight.

All eyes change with age, and it is usual to see a clouding over of the pupil. This can be either due to cataracts, or due to nuclear sclerosis. To the naked eye, both look very similar, and just because the pupil is becoming cloudy, it doesn't mean that the dog cannot see.

Nuclear sclerosis is simply a condensing of the components that make up the lens, and dogs can see through this. Cataracts also affect the lens; however, they are completely opaque and will lead to blindness of the dog. A veterinarian will be able to distinguish between the two by looking into the eye with an ophthalmoscope.

If a dog becomes blind, it is usually a slow process, which gives the owner time to start training useful commands, such as "wait," "slowly," and "step."

Many dogs will also lose their hearing. Since there are very few tests that can be done to assess hearing in pets, the extent to which an individual has lost its hearing is somewhat subjective. You might start to think your dog is becoming naughty and not responding to commands, but actually he just has not heard the command. When teaching commands as a puppy, it is a good idea to also teach a hand signal, so that he will also respond to this when he can no longer hear. For his safety, though, in open or public spaces, it is a good idea to keep your dog on a leash, as his recall will no longer be existent.

Bladder Control

Photo Courtesy of Stephanie Chung

Bladder control is something that many female dogs may struggle with when they become elderly. It is common for a spayed female to lose some control of their bladder, as estrogen plays a major role in tightening the sphincter at the exit of the bladder. Therefore, if the dog has not had many hormones during its life, then the bladder can possibly leak later on in life.

Another major cause of bladder leakage or loss of control is when the dog has arthritis in the lumbosacral area of the spine. The nerves that come out of the spinal cord in this area are the ones which innervate the sphincter and bladder muscles. Compression of these nerves will lead to loss of control.

Determining the root cause of the loss of bladder control is essential when it comes to treatment. There are several medications available which help improve bladder control if it is due to lack of hormones, but if the reason is due to the back, then very little can be done.

It is important that if urine leaks excessively, then the area is bathed at least once daily to stop urine scald, and the hair is kept short in that area for hygiene reasons. Doggy diapers are also available.

CHAPTER 15   Living with a Senior Dog

Saying Goodbye

When it comes to the end of a dog's life, saying goodbye can be one of the hardest things an owner will ever have to do. Sometimes the time is very clear cut, and the dog has deteriorated extremely quickly. Other times, the time is less evident, for example with chronic and advanced arthritis, where the dog is much the same from one day to the next. In these times, it is important to consider the dog's quality of life. This can be done through asking some basic questions:

1. Is he still happy and wagging his tail on a regular basis?
2. Is he still keen to eat?
3. Does he still interact how he used to?
4. Can he still perform normal day-to-day activities?

If the answer to any of those is no, then the quality of life is compromised, and depending on the reason and prognosis, it may be the best option to consider euthanasia (also known as putting the dog to sleep).

Euthanasia is often perceived as a terrible thing for owners and dogs alike; however, most people agree afterward that it is actually peaceful and they are grateful to the veterinarian to enable their dog to stop suffering. The procedure is simply an overdose of anesthetic, which as the name suggests, simply puts the dog into a very deep sleep from which they slip away. It is quick at under 15 seconds, and completely pain free. Most veterinarians have a routine they are familiar with, which allows the whole process to be very smooth.

When the time comes, it can be done at home by calling a vet to the house, or it can be done in the car in the veterinary practice's parking lot, or alternatively in the consulting room. Some vets give the injection straight from a needle, whereas others prefer inserting a cannula first, especially if the blood pressure is poor and finding a vein is not going to be an easy process. There may be some muscle twitching after the injection, or a reflex which causes the dog to look like he is taking a deep breath, but these are natural things which happen after the dog has passed away, so they are not indications that something has gone wrong. The veterinarian will confirm the passing by checking for a heartbeat with a stethoscope.

Many veterinary practices will offer cremation or disposal services if the owner does not want to take the dog home for burial.

Saying goodbye can be extremely tough; however, it is important to look back on the amazing life and joy that your little Yorkshire Terrier has brought to your household, and celebrate your dog's life, as well as be grateful for all the special times spent together over those years.

ACKNOWLEDGMENTS

Without the presence of my little family Yorkie, Paddy, much of this book would only be written with professional knowledge, but Paddy-Paws has allowed me to learn everything there is to know about Yorkshire Terriers from firsthand experience. He is a bouncy, cheeky little mister, and even at his ripe old age, people think he is still a little puppy. He has brought the whole family so much joy, and I'm sure your Yorkie will too.

I would also like to thank Clare Hardy for her professional input on this book, both for her Yorkshire Terrier knowledge and for her contributions to editing the final manuscript. Her contribution has been invaluable.

www.ingramcontent.com/pod-product-compliance
Lightning Source LLC
Chambersburg PA
CBHW060044230426
43661CB00004B/643